Working

Your Way

Up the Corporation

WORKING
YOUR WAY
UP THE CORPORATION

Charles Murrah

SHERBOURNE PRESS, INC.
LOS ANGELES

Library of Congress Catalog Card Number 00-000

ISBN 0-8202-0124-3

FIRST PRINTING

Composition: Chapman's Phototypesetting, Fullerton, Calif.
Printed and bound by R.R. Donnelley & Sons, Crawfordsville, Ind.

Contents

causes him to refrain from doing his own thing. Such laughter in effect says to that man, "How can you be so stupid?"

8. UPPER LEVELING

Because so many of my bosses would pigeonhole ideas coming up from below, I had to find ways to float my thoughts and concepts around them.

9. GOOD NEWSITIS

When giving out dope to stockholders, customers, competitors, and the general public, good news is thought to be worth its weight in gold. Therefore, when there is anything bad to be dished out, it is very likely coupled with something at least hopeful, if not definitely good.

10. SOPPING

No recruiting process sets the limit on where the job can lead. Limitations might dampen the spirit of the guy being brought in to fill it. In fact, you can be passed over for promotion three times and be put on a permanent shelf, and nobody, but nobody, is about to tell you your future is not bright. Sopping, then, is a way of life in big business.

11. SALARY SUCTION

It is the suction upward of each job level's pay rate on the one below it that compounds the compensation problem and runs up the cost of management, often out of all proportion to its worth.

12. FIRST GUESSING

Lucky me. I had sprouted my eyeteeth in the army, where protecting one's rear becomes a way of life, so I brought an instinct into business for blocking off blame. But I also knew about the valuable trophies that risk taking can throw off when things go right.

13. PYRAMIDING

In business, the height of one's platform is greatly determined by what management up the line thinks about him, but the strength of his position has more to do with what the people down below think.

Foreword

MY TWENTY-TWO YEARS of scratching for success, power, money, and personal satisfaction in business constitute the research upon which this book is based. I entered a big corporation at the bottom and came out the length of a cat's whisker from the top. Therefore, the reader can measure the wisdom I had at the start against my final insight, forged by a successful, satisfying experience.

If it is true that a person's character at any given moment is largely controlled by his experiences, then you may get a preview of the kind of person you could become by the close of your business career, since it is most unlikely that the nature of corporate life will change so rapidly that your experiences will be totally different from mine.

Whether you are a young tiger burning brightly or an older war horse nearing the ultimate rewards of your labors, there is still time to change as a personality before the end of your business life. It is never too early or too late to ask yourself, "What will my business career do to me?" rather than the usual question, "What can I do to further my own position?" It is a rare person who doesn't end up as the product of what the business did to him instead of what he did to himself in pursuit of his own good. Yet, few people ever measure the impact of the corporation upon themselves: they prefer to measure their influence upon the company in terms of power and money. Most business people lose sight of the fact that their experiences are often triggered by the actions of others rather than by their own deeds; therefore, their behavior is not entirely self-determined.

On your trip through these pages, why not concentrate on what your company is doing to you instead of dwelling upon what your next move might be to get ahead? If you will, you just might learn something about the guy or gal you'll become by the time you pass the baton of your career to another. It's important to remember that when that time comes, each departed will be forced to live with what he is, while the person to whom the baton is passed will be free to cut a different pattern.

I'll leave it up to you to judge my degree of contentment as I left the corporate scene, just as I'll be compelled to let you measure your own feelings of joy over your present position in business and what effect it is having on you. Happy reading on your way to a happy life is my wish for every reader.

1

EVERLASTING CORPORATE LIFE

DANGLING FROM THE end of a single thread of life, I dip into the pools of people making up society to find my bread and air and water. In exchange for the life-giving things I take, I am expected to put some effort into the pot. But no pool should rely on me for much, for I can be gone in a flash. In fact, each part of society must set up a system to take the sting out of any man's death. The social unit known as business has come up with the corporation as its tool for keeping the impact of death a minor matter. In a corporation, the death of an owner or a manager does not shut down the company. Such a business, then, can have everlasting life. So can a country. So can an army. So can a church. So can a charity. You name it; properly managed, a pool of people can have a long life.

In my mind, there was a hell of a guy swinging on the little thread of life assigned to me. Lucky would be the ponds in which I would decide to swim. Scratching out my own spot in the ground had its charm, but easing down into a big-business wallowing hole seemed more safe. I was aware that I would be a small fish in a big puddle, but my energy, drive, and desire would lead me to a big splash. So I touched down into a three and a half billion dollar company, ready to change the system for the better and to find my road to personal happiness. As one of thousands, I was in a great spot to show the world that I was some special kind of human being. To do so, I had to seek a seat of power.

The company was into its second century of everlasting life when I joined up. How the hell it got there without me, I never bothered to ask. It had me now; how lucky could it get? I most surely expected to have a deep effect on where it went. To do so, I had to have a seat of power. It didn't take me long to make a move to grab some strength. The crud of the ages was lying all about. No genius was needed to see the chances for new ways to do the old jobs better. Before I warmed my seat well, I began to tell the old guard what needed to be done. What a shock! To me, not to them. One guy said he had spent more time in the cafeteria than I was likely to spend with the company. Another stuck his finger in a glass of water and pulled it out, saying that I'd leave that kind of a hole if I dropped dead. The lamp shades seemed far more lasting than I, as far as the old-timers were concerned.

Not being quite as stupid as I was conceited, I started to look for ways to work with the people, to find my power base. Some way had to be found to draw on all that money and all those people to make my own mark. It became a challenge not to get lost in the shuffle and, most decidedly, not to turn tail and run. The company was a big pond, somewhat polluted of course, but one could scarcely find a better place to seek his fortune, both in money and in deeds. So hanging from my own little thread of life, I began to swim with the tides, not against them. The prime tide was the sheer bigness of the outfit, and I had to learn to become part of it, not to buck it. That company wasn't going to cut down its size just to make me feel more important. In fact, I wanted to make it bigger in my own self-interest, but if I couldn't roll with the bigness, it would crush me.

Tide number two in my personal adjustment was realizing that the company didn't need me. My quarters in the everlasting barracks of big business were temporary, and keeping me housed there was not a company objective. Oh, the company needed somebody like me, but it didn't need *me*. It was a blow to my ego to admit this, but I was temporary; the company had the everlasting life. My business life would be but a blip on the radar screen of the company's existence. How could a man with so much pride be happy where the lamp shades did indeed outlast most of the people? I had to accept it and not take myself so seriously. My sanity and physical well-being would depend on it. Also, if I was personally tense, I would add to the tension around the company, thus slowing things down, and I wanted to speed things up, in the interest of tucking my power base up underneath me. I would serve my economic lord and master, the company, in the interest of its everlasting life, and would literally laugh myself through my small portion of the outfit's total days.

In terms of total days, how many did I have? At age thirty, I had 12,775 to go to age sixty-five. Only two-thirds would be working days, and only one-third of each working day was work. One-third of two-thirds is only one-sixth of the time from any age to age sixty-five. I could hardly afford to screw up my whole life for just one-sixth of the time. Not only was I a temporary soul in the everlasting life of my company, I was a part-timer as well. I resolved that whatever ulcers, coronaries, and lower-back pains I got would come from something other than working. If I really did come up with a seat of power, it would not be through worshiping at an altar on which my own burnt flesh was sacrificed.

Herein lies the key to corporate happiness; there comes a time when waste and lack of talent are no longer bothersome. I saw the presence of these things as my greatest personal asset. The weakness of the system and the limited energies of the people in it would give me the chance to stand out in the crowd, without wearing myself out. Within the eight-hour day for the two-thirds working time in the year, I could gain enough power to suit me and not even breathe hard. The everlasting corporate body could chug along at its modest pace, and I could hang my goose to a lofty limb, stuff him with money like a horn of plenty, and end up eating off his carcass for the rest of my life. Let's face it, a talent like mine was well served to have a slow pace in which to cut its mustard and to build its castles. Without it, I would not have attained the power, position, and income that I did.

Don't get me wrong; I tried my best to speed things up, and so did many other men. Many things were improved, but the size of the challenge in the modern-day world grows faster than do the abilities of the people charged with facing it. This situation was tide number three: expanding difficulties of doing business in the face of less expanding talents among the work force. After twenty-two years, I found myself part of the slow pace and not in front of it. In spite of my many remarks over those years about the system and its lack of an ability to vault ahead, I finally found myself running behind the everlasting corporate body in my own capacity. The young tigers joining up today see in me the same hindrance that I saw years ago in the old guys who wouldn't knuckle under to my instant answers to old problems. Man is a temporary being and ends up proving it by falling apart, while a corporation can live forever and end up better in itself than any single man who joins it. As a young man, I made my company better than the old guys going out had done. As I go out, there are young men all over the company making it better than this old guy ever would have.

So, tiger, young or old, your company is going to plow you under, one of these days. This fact won't bother you if you can accept it right now and fight your battles with it in mind. I recommend that you ride the tide of bigness, knowing how very unnecessary you are and that the day will come when the wave will wash you up on the beach and leave you there. If you are earnest in your efforts, you can piggyback on top of the company's everlasting life and ride about as high as you want to ride. But there are certain rules you'll have to follow and definite games you'll have to play. The question is whether or not you want to be a part of bigness. If you do, you'll have to observe the rules and play the games. While the youth of today face different challenges and live in a new world, there is really no change in the people-to-people living conditions in corporate life. As I move aside, it is clear that the conduct of men in business changes slowly and that people tackle today's operational duties with just about the same human character traits as were used when I started out. As human beings, we are little changed in twenty years. Thus, the future is going to be about like the past, as far as basic conduct is concerned, no matter how many changes in methods of doing business come along. These past, and almost sure to be future, patterns of human conduct are what this book is all about.

Don't let me discourage you from trying to change them. Some need badly to go by the wayside. I'm really hoping that reading about them will give you some insight into how to make new patterns of human behavior. But I would be going against my twenty-two years of experience if I pushed you to do what I really couldn't do myself. So I'm working harder on trying to show you how to ride with the punches and to avoid discouragement when the same old game gets played in your part of your company's everlasting life. You'll change its processes and its profits more if you'll adapt to its rules for human conduct in the interest of bettering its end result, rather than try to put in a new set of day-to-day living conditions. In any event, you should know about the old rules and the old games.

Working under those rules and playing those games, I had many a thrill. I stood like Custer from time to time and, on two occasions, barely escaped his fate. I appeared before large groups of company people and left the platform to much applause. I earned the power I sought, to almost the degree that I sought it. I earned money far in excess of my beginning goals, though I developed a huge appetite later, which didn't get filled. I fell in and out of step with top management, only to survive each crisis. I even left a couple of operational bequests to the future, which could be around for a hundred years. Oh yes, I had my thrills all right, but there is no getting away from the fact that the company would be in just about the exact same place today if it had never laid eyes on me. That's the galling side of *everlasting corporate life* to an individual man. Big business takes our frontiers away and lets us conquer little. In fact, it tends to conquer us and shoves its everlasting life down our throats, hollering, "Take it or leave it," as it goes on about its way.

No wonder there is always the cry to change the system. The establishment is a threat to the young, and big business is the most dire threat of all. Religion at least says to man, "You're going to live forever." Big business says, "I'm going to live forever. You're going to dip down here for your daily bread, last a while if you're man enough to stand the gaff, and die without ever having chopped down a single windmill." Few men see such a future as the kind to get excited about, but most have to spend their lives doing just what big business says. To tell you that I didn't would be a lie, but I can say with a perfectly straight face that I did have fun doing it. I repeat, and do not lie, when I say that I laughed my way through twenty-two years, while watching other men chew themselves up something fierce.

Looking back, I can see that I did give the company two pretty good things to talk about. One, I came on board and brought a fresh, new personality to liven up the scene. Two, I left and took away my preconceived notions and my dislike for certain people. In between, there were many benefits for me and much work done. I was able to accept my place in the scheme of things and did get put in a series of jobs which suited me. My little piece of the company's everlasting life went happily by in a hurry. Read on if there is a chance in a million that you may spend part of your working life in a big company.

2

ALL-UPMANSHIP

DID YOU EVER stunt around in a tennis match or showboat on some athletic field? Then you know that coaches scream at one-upmanship. "Don't be bush," they say. Corporations give ground grudgingly to stunters, too. Rugged individuals are expected to polish off their personal urges when they join the team. Every company brings some in to chew on. To swallow or not to swallow is the question. Tigers taste good, but it takes guts to handle them. Not all companies have the stomach for it. Ruminants have a way of managing this digestive problem. They chew a while, swallow into stomach number one to test toughness, cough up and chew some more, or spit out on the ground.

Here's what you have to decide. If you are going to stay in big business, you must learn to cope with "all-upmanship." It takes the place of one-man shows. Teams are formed at all levels of a company. There is the super-team at the top, which you cannot ignore, but in your early days with the outfit, you'll be more wrapped up with smaller teams.

Leaders in all ranks will be getting ready to vault ahead. Sadly, they cannot do so unless they are able to put teams together. You can have the concentration of Bobby Fischer, the physical power of Dick Butkus, and the looks of Burt Reynolds, but you're not going anywhere on the strength of your own merits. Each of the guys vying for promotion will be trying to line up his forces. First, you'll find yourself being coaxed into the orbit of some man above you. Next, you'll find out about the tiers of teams as some dandy above your boss will start shining to dazzle you. Then will come the day when you have to start making motions to rally your supporters from lower down. It takes all three of these steps before you will begin to see how much of your life is going to be spent in being lined up for teams and in lining up your own. If all of this effort was spent on work, most companies could reduce their staffs by twenty percent, but the reasons for the existence of teams will never disappear. Therefore, the team system will not disappear either.

If a team stunts around and goofs, there are too many involved to throw out the group. Let a lone man screw up, and he can go. Therefore, you learn early to hold your risky moves to team projects. Without this safety, all men would stand around with their thumbs up their butts and do nothing for fear of failure. See why teams can't possibly disappear? This aspect alone wouldn't be so bad. Companies must take risks, and more than one mind should be used to decide on big things. Teams make people talk things out and give them the guts to act. It's the God-awful political side of all-upmanship that makes teams a threat to companies. The pangs of team birth, the arrogance of team victory, and the throes of team death drain off the juices of a company and clog the system.

Your first attempt to put a team together will open your eyes to the raw truth that everything has to be done under cover. If you talk to a man about his joining you to further your future and his own, you will have his instant lip service. He cannot brush you off until he knows for sure that you are going nowhere. But you can make these flimsy deals with half the crowd and not be certain of a single soul's support in the clutch. Then will dawn a frightening thought: the guys trying to add you to their teams cannot be sure of you either. The bond of personal commitment that we Americans like to see in ourselves is just not there. It's not a pleasant experience to gaze into the mirror and see a man who knows he must go through life feigning loyalty to many men, while keeping his feet in the starting blocks to spring past those very same men at the right moment. But, tiger, this is exactly where it's at. Get ready to join many teams and to head up your own.

The things that bosses up the line will do to bind you to them will be the training grounds on which they teach you to put a team together. If I were one of these men, here are some ways that I could lock you up, for now, on my team. I could give you a spotlight-type duty—put you in charge of a committee or something out of step with your past record. You could head up a special group with guys senior to you having to report to you for the project. (As an army captain, I once had three light colonels reporting to me; I would have charged a pillbox single-handedly for the general who gave me that thrill.) I could approve the things you want to do and turn down the men of your same rank. You can hardly think my leadership stinks when I'm giving you your head on most of your ideas. I can put my good word about your work on the grapevine, sending it up and down. If my boss stops you in the hall and tells you that I am singing your praises, you start to get a warm feeling about me as a boss. Beginning to see how to do it? I have tied you to me without either of us saying a word. Believe me, I'll be back for my pound of flesh.

I was knighted into the home office from the field fourteen years ago. My title was modest and my salary was in the high teens, but there were only five job levels above me in the entire company. As I step out, there are still five jobs bigger than mine, but my salary has tripled and my title is vice president. What kind of fool am I? Certainly not fool enough to drop off that kind of team early in the game. The knights in shining armor are good at that. They

delight in all-upping the crowd in title and salary to keep
the Whiz Kids happy. As for me, I was making the same con-
tribution, five layers from the top, but I sure as hell wasn't
enjoying it any less walking around on those thick carpets
and sitting behind that flying boxcar of a desk. Top management saw me as part of its team. I mounted the corporate
ladder and got promoted so many times that I lost count,
only to find that my feet were still planted on the same rung.
I felt like the radio operator who got the Bronze Star for
sending and receiving many messages with utter disregard
for his own personal safety, from a dugout no less.

Are you beginning to see how teams get formed? Are
you getting a clammy feeling as you see how people with
little talent can get far in rank by teaming up with the right
guy? Do you see how many men with large abilities to work
well can get nowhere due to their lack of a flair for team
dealing? If you happen to be one who does not want to
play a team role, can you be content to take your corporate
chances on your raw talent, or will you have to change your
views to fit the system? Much is heard about getting caught
up in the corporate rat race. Men are always saying how
much they hate to get caught, as if one had no choice. But
there is a choice; the rat race can be avoided. All one has
to do is to refuse to line up with the team idea. Fly as a loner,
and you can stay out of the rat race.

The rewards for staying out of the team system are
great in such areas as personal pride, social freedom,
respect from the low-level people, and release from job pressure; but if you want a measure of such joys in your business life, be prepared to pay a price in dollars for the right
to have them. As hard as it is to accept, a big company can
find scads of men with your ability. It puts you in its mainstream because it thinks you have the thing called drive,
not because it thinks you can work. The minute you show
no desire to fight for team leadership or to thrill at being a
part of somebody else's team, you are written off as a man

with a very limited future. It's as though no man can be considered fit for a job unless he is willing to stake his all on getting it. The man at the top, who did risk much to get his slot, cannot put another in a big job on merit alone. He had to fight; everybody else must too. Stay out of the rat race if you like, but be prepared to spend your corporate life working quietly at a modest job level—not calling shots from the top.

Because of these circumstances, most men elect to play the team game. The trick is to get on the right team at the start and to line up the right people under you as you get far enough along to make up a team of your own. Be careful to stay underground as long as possible with your outward support, but be sure you tie yourself to winning leadership by deeds, in time for the leader to know you are on his team. Otherwise, you may find yourself out in the cold, suspected of being loyal to the beaten side. If the team in charge writes you off, you will feel the direct effect of its arrogance. When a man is shooting for a big job, he is decent to just about everybody. Let him win, and he hides no likes or dislikes. The people he likes are put in key spots, and the ones he has no use for are placed in minor roles. The talent in the crowd has almost nothing to do with who is put in what spot. The new Mr. Big is far more concerned with how much personal support he will get from you in the future than with your ability. Too bad, tiger, that's the way it is. When you made the decision to get with the team idea, you placed your desire to excel as a worker behind your willingness to seek personal progress as a semikept man. That's when you got caught up in the corporate rat race and started the churning that comes from giving up one's unique self.

You usually have to spend some time both in and out of favor, if you hang around a company very long. Few are shrewd enough to win consistently for twenty or more years. You should prepare yourself to be in some of the time and out some. When you are out, learn to deal with revenge. When in, learn how to keep your own arrogance under control. Every winning leader struts to some degree. Before he starts to reap any true benefit from his new power, he lashes out with some crappy act of dominance to rub the noses of the fallen in the dirt. He'll call a meeting and parade his team; he'll call a halt to the work being done by the key guys who had the gall to oppose him in his quest for the job. Some heads will roll; others will flee. Who goes or who stays will be of no consequence. All that will matter is the willingness of those who stay to rally round the flag of the new boss. Is this the way you want to go through life? In any event, make a conscious choice. Don't just let the system handle you; work the system.

In my early years, I had a ball, acting as if I had the drive of a buffalo on the make. All day long, I showed the urge to vault ahead, but at the end of the day, I walked out of the building under no pressure, to get my kicks as a loner away from business. I knocked my work out in less time than was expected to give the impression that the teams I knew were forming could count on me. There is nothing better than meeting deadlines and turning in well-thought-out paperwork to make leaders think that they have your all-out support. However, all the time, there was a casual air about me that seemed out of step with the drive I showed in getting my work done. This made all the guys up the line want me around, but kept them off balance, never knowing when I might start some power play of my own. This mystery gave them the urge to keep me moving ahead at a good pace but not fast enough to be an unexpected threat to them. My title and salary got bigger and bigger, though my role never really changed. My work was fun, and I did reap big team benefits without having to throw away too much of myself in the process.

Over the years, however, the desire to quit acting like a team member got very strong. Having watched all-upmanship in motion for so long, I decided to junk my identity as a team man, to seek some form of power generating out of my talent alone. This decision meant that I had to quit. There is no way to remain at the vice-presidential level in corporate life, after openly declaring unwillingness to work with the team idea. It's as impossible to stay ahead on merit as it is to get ahead on merit. Management cannot tolerate anything but blind loyalty from its officers. In fact, the more talent a man has, the less he can be allowed to do his own thing. Don't be fooled by one of today's top management exercises—the so-called open door policy. What good is an open door in front of a closed mind? Team members who state their individual views have a way of dropping out of sight. The day I decided to come out into the open with my dislike of teams is the day I decided to retire.

Another reason I wanted out was the impending death of the team to which I belonged. The throes of its passing were going to be more than I wanted to sit through. Due to the long time that the top man had been in power, none of the men sitting around hoping to take over had ever had to show much ability to manage the company. They were just like me, untested and not steeled by responsibility. All that was really known about them was their team loyalty. The top man had held them in his hip pocket so long that the final ravages of all-upmanship could not be avoided. On his way out, he would promote them all, splinter top authority, and hang around in the wings himself to keep some semblance of order. Not being the least bit inclined to hide my distrust of this inevitable occurrence, I retired.

Read the newspapers about retirements and watch the lines of succession that are set up. You'll see such things as chairman of the executive committee, chairman, vice chairman, interim president, president, and three or four new executive vice presidents. Mr. Big got off in a room by himself and knuckled under to the urge to prepare one last feast for everybody. Rest assured that he plans to keep his own feet under the table. After all those years of telling men to give up their individuality for the good of the company, his own private brand of one-upmanship takes charge of him to make him think he's still needed. All-upmanship has now, in his case, come down to what it really is—the act of using other people to serve one's own desire to stunt around.

3

YOUTHANASIA

IN A WARTIME army, nobody cares how fast the young get promoted. "Colonels under the age of twenty-three will not be served beer before three o'clock in the afternoon," made a funny sign in an officers' club in World War II. Once the dying stops and things get back to normal, people quit laughing about the fast progress of youth. Big business is a place where quick-moving young hot shots are never a laughing matter. Experience never moves around youth; it's always the other way. Zooming out of nowhere comes a young squirt to grab off a plum of a job right under the nose of a man who has spent fifteen years getting ready for just that spot. "Youthanasia" has struck. The young guy sees his promotion as part of management's wisdom. The older man sees the nonmercy killing of his career. Both need some kind of insight into themselves if they expect to be happy in corporate life.

I have vaulted over the stretched-out bodies of older men and landed on the other side singing Glory, Glory, Hallelujah before they knew what hit them. I have promoted a younger man over a more qualified man just because the older guy didn't look the part I wanted him to play in the setup. I have also stood up for an older man when my own boss was dead set against his rise in rank—with success, I'm happy to say. I have threatened to resign if the boss didn't promote the older man I wanted, only to chicken out when he told me to go to hell. I have been jumped over by a young man whose great personality made management give him a job that I wanted with a passion. I have held the hand of my own boss when he could hardly talk after swallowing the bitter pill of seeing a young guy go around him. No matter which side of the youthanasia coin one is on, he needs some kind of inner strength to cope.

It dawned on me early in my business career that being in a certain job could be bad for me, that I could get hurt by what I got. Out of this discovery came an understanding that the jobs I didn't get could never hurt me. I learned to dwell on the power and the glory of not becoming something. Surely there is power and glory in more title and more money, and I never got my fill of either, but the only personal power and glory that my boss has that I don't have is his power and glory over me. As a person, I can touch any life that he can touch. As a person, I can resist any temptation that he can resist. As a person, I have power and glory over him matching his power and glory over me, which makes us equal. Therefore, no other man's promotion can put me down, nor can my own promotion put me up. I can put myself down by getting upset over another man's good luck, but that putdown is minor compared to the one I can get if I happen to stumble into a job that my own personality will not fit. In other words, I had better hope that my management keeps me out of jobs that are not right for me.

I have seen men get the job of their dreams, only to yearn early for the power and the glory of not having that particular job. A young man I know of was sponsored by a big boss and put in a key slot in a department—not knowing that the department head did not want him. The young fellow was able to do the job well, but ruffled feathers showed up all over the landscape. The department head took credit for the improvements and succeeded in making a villain out of the young man who did the work. When the young man was removed from the job, the top, top cat who started the whole thing was as silent as a mouse. A few minutes with that young man could give one a pretty good understanding of the power and the glory of not becoming something. Even his absolute success at the duty could not save him.

In another case, a strong department head was moved up to bigger things and not replaced by a man of like rank. Instead, top management reached far down into the outfit and put a very junior man in charge. He was so junior that promoting him all the way to the level of the job was quite an error. He vaulted over a big crew of older guys and had to burn the midnight oil to keep ahead of them. One night after the supply of oil was gone, he piloted his high-powered car into an abutment and instant death. The extra time required to get on top of his job could have been part of the fatigue that made him go to sleep at the wheel. His family understands what the power and the glory of not becoming something might have meant.

My corporate goal was to be in charge of sales. When age fifty went hurtling by without my making it, the curtain came down for good on my advancement. I was a full vice president in the department, with the same rank as the guy in charge of sales, but I never had the final word. Something in my personality kept management from wanting me in that job. Never have I had to call on the power and the glory of not becoming something quite as I did when this job got away, but now I can applaud the wisdom that wouldn't let me have it. Had I gotten it, there is no way that I would be happily enjoying my new career as a retired guy doing a wide variety of things. I could not have given up the sales job I so badly wanted.

Youthanasia takes its toll on both the young and the old, unless each can find his own right attitude to the conditions it forces upon him. As a young guy on the move, I found it hard to manage a man after passing over him. I had to become an expert in the tattle-tale gray signs of slacking off by the older man. He may start coming in late and leaving early. He will stop taking his briefcase home after years of extra work away from the job. His handwriting will suddenly become sloppy, where neatness has been his former stock-in-trade. At first, I jumped in with both feet to straighten out the old codger. He and I would go round and round, with me promising to take action if his attitude didn't improve. After about two tries with this tactic, I began to feel like Omar Bradley trying to tell George Patton how to smile. I soon learned that my job was not to make such a man happy but to see that he worked. That's when I started to schedule him, deadline him, check up on his daily output, and give him special projects to stretch him out. He could literally growl at me, if he kept on top of his work. As long as he worked, his griping was a sign to my bosses that I could keep an old passed-over man productive. Had I flunked this test, my bosses would have never moved me around many experienced people.

Many young tigers flunk this test and allow the fifty- and sixty-year-old guys to stack up in the back rooms at high pay and reduced effort. Such old guys go to sleep and make a project out of bitching at the management. It's the "They can pass me over but they can't make me like it" attitude. If one of them died, the company would hardly miss him, but lying around half-asleep makes him a drag. The largest single raise in pay rate that a man ever gets in business is the one he gives himself. It comes when he decides to cut back on his output and to stop fighting for future raises. Bosses are the last to know when this decision is made. A guy can slack off by twenty-five percent and few supervisors can see the difference—possibly the difference between making a profit or losing money.

Unions are forever damned for cutting back on output. It's easy to count the bricks they lay, the tonnage they move, the buttons they sew on. Managers behind desks in big business are not subject to any such count. Those that are passed over and pissed off by youthanasia sit behind those desks and make union members look like solid citizens in the fight against inflation. Youth's movement through big business has a deep effect on the wage-price spiral when it piles up big groups of older people, drawing big pay at low production. Every young man who jumps ahead should try hard to get a full day's work out of the aging men whose spirits were broken by not being put in charge, but it is easier for youth to back itself up with more youth and to compound the problem, adding to the stack of old guys in the back rooms.

As time took its toll, I began to lose enthusiasm for more title, and young men started moving around me. Remembering when the shoe was on the other foot, I did my best not to fall back in effort. I stepped up my work to avoid being a problem for the young tiger who now had to see that I carried my weight. I tried hard to remain pleasant, although I didn't always succeed. Bitching openly was not for me, and I never asked top management why I did not get the job. Some of my bosses brushed up beside me to see how I was taking the blow; I am proud to brag that none heard a peep out of me. Try it, you'll like it, and you will begin to feel the power and the glory of not becoming something.

A well-known sports program on television talks about the thrill of victory and the agony of defeat. Youthanasia in big business is a vivid example of what that program is all about. If all races were ties, none would be run. The road to the top in any company is a rat-race track. I ran the race expecting to jump over bodies along the way. Top management had to provide the open path that allowed me to run for the roses and had to deal with the let-down souls over which I leaped. Having been the "jumper" and the "jumped," I know that one man's triumph can be another man's career death. Every man who starts out on that rat-race track today needs some inner source of personal strength to help him handle the highs of his life without arrogance and the lows without self-defeating pain.

Look carefully at pictures of champions. The thrill of victory and the agony of defeat appear so clearly in but a single shot. The champ exults, and the beaten suffers, whether he is in the picture or not. When my face started showing up in the company newspaper after I won the prize of promotion, I had no feeling for the man who wasn't there; but when I suddenly became the man who wasn't there, I got to know how much grief my many successes had spread around. The receiving end of youthanasia is not a happy spot.

The most vivid picture that I have ever seen about the thrill of victory and the agony of defeat is the one showing the Marines as they stuck up the flag on Mount Surabachi at the end of the battle for Iwo Jima. At great personal risk, a photographer recorded the thrill of victory, and he did so beautifully. But it was the dead on the slopes, not in the picture, who supplied the agony. Death gave credibility to the whole idea. The sequel to the picture is wrapped up in the fact that so few of those men made it back to the States. One who did lost his personal perspective as a result of hero worship and died a tragic death at a very young age. His loved ones could talk at length about the power and the glory of not becoming something. If power or glory invades a man's person, he is no good to himself or his company. Youthanasia puts both the young and the old to the test in this regard.

4

WHOLLY GHOSTING

THERE ARE MANY bibles on corporate management, and all issue this commandment in some form: "Thou shalt not rely upon thyself alone in making decisions, nor shalt thou always have thine own way." The guys who write the books have never worn the crown. What could they tell me about the practical side of my duties? I had the brain, the drive, and the desire for success demanded by my position. Otherwise, the company would not have put me there. My outfit would go as far as I could take it. So here I came, dragging my people behind me. I asked for advice but hardly heard it. I read reports, but doubted the dope. I reread the corporate bible and then burned it. I knew how to swim—to hell with the waterwings of asking others what to do. The unit reporting to me lost its voice in its own destiny.

How did the unit react? It cut off its supply of information to me. Even worse, it started telling me only what it wanted me to know. Experience lay around idle. Valuable knowledge went underground. I was failing the basic test and breaking the commandment. It suddenly became very important to lull the outfit into thinking that I wanted its ideas in decision-making. Here's when I first learned the ways of "wholly ghosting." My conceit led me to believe that it was a personal invention, but its use is widespread among business leaders at all levels. The technique is simple.

You start using people, programs, and projects to put on an act. You act as if you are using all the information and experience on hand, without really doing so.

How's this for cuteness? Having made up my mind to promote a certain man, I asked for figures showing what ten percent more business in his specialty would have done to improve our overall unit cost. As I knew, the impact would have been great. Then I asked the sales promotion guy whether or not such an increase was possible. "Hell yeah!" he said. And so on around the horn. By asking for worthless dope, I found it easy to fake the use of other people in making my one-man decision. Not one ounce of true knowledge had to be brought to bear nor a single bit of experience called on. I wholly ghosted the people into thinking they were part and parcel of my individual act. Make you want to puke? It did me, too. Before many months went by, I was having coughs, colds, a sore asshole, and pimples in the eyebrows.

This early brush made me resolve not to use ghosting in decision-making. It also kept me alert to the wholly ghosting of management over me. At parties and on the train with commuting buddies, the topic was often discussed. Needless to say, my company had no monopoly on its use, and many were quick to volunteer examples. I found many of them using ghosts, being ghosts themselves, and having friends in the host of corporate ghosts. It was clear that my future would be much involved with this ghost bit. It was, and I served my time as a ghost.

A friend gave me this little gem on how a boss can plant a ghost to shape minds. Joe said to Bill, "I was talking to Mr. Powerful the other day in Chattanooga, and he thinks we should have an office in California." Next day, Joe said to Aaron, "Going home last night, Mr. Big was saying how much he hates to go to Lubbock." Later on in the week, Joe went to some little guy who had the book on economic growth and got some numbers on potential sales in

San Diego versus actual sales in Lubbock. The boss, meanwhile, was put on the board of his old junior college in San Diego. At the meeting to consider the matter, Bill said, "You know, sir, we don't have an office west of the Rockies." Aaron chirped, "I'd be against opening one unless we closed one someplace else." Joe got out his figures on San Diego's promise and Lubbock's bad sales record. Man, that office is on its way to California. Mr. Big said that he took the advice of the operating boys who recommended the move. All together, but not too loud, "Fiddlesticks!" Joe ghosted, Bill and Aaron soldiered, and the old man got what he wanted. My friend said that Joe, Bill, and Aaron were really sweating it out, for the boss was sure to blame them if things went wrong in San Diego. Such is the risk that ghosts take, along with the chance that their coworkers will learn not to trust them. In spite of the risks, people do serve their time as ghosts.

I had one very painful tour of duty as a ghost. The top management was bound and determined to start a mutual fund. Not being interested in the sale of equity-based products, I told my boss that the company should not involve me. I am so fixed-dollar minded that pushing the sale of mutual funds would go against my grain, making me wholly unfit to take an active part in the project. Within a week, I was made president of our mutual fund sales outlet—my one chance to be president of something, and it had to be as a ghost. I was told that somebody had to sign the papers; top management knew that I was a life insurance man posing as an equity-products expert. We had at least a year to wait for government approval; I could learn all about selling funds in that much time. Besides, the guys in the field were straining at the bit to get going on sales. There was really no reason for me to worry; not knowing my butt from first base about mutual funds was no sweat. On top of all that, my primary job was not to be changed. The fund thing was an in-addition-to type duty.

And so it was, until the fund hit the field, and the men out there showed a great lack of interest in its sale. Top management started asking this fairly competent life insurance man, posing as wholly-a-ghost of a securities salesman, where the heck sales were. Nobody had to tell me who had the bug on his back to move that product. It was me, pure and simple. Simple I was, pure, no. I know now that nothing on earth should have influenced me to accept the sales job for mutual funds. I also know that one becomes a ghost when he lets himself be used. My continuing distaste out of this affair is with myself. Had I been really concerned about the proper decision, I would not have allowed myself to be made a ghost. My heart goes out to all men starting out in corporate life. It's not easy to say no to anything that bosses direct one to do. Soldiering is the order of the day, but it can lead to death as well as medals.

Not only can individuals be ghosts, sizeable parts of a company can be made to serve a ghosting function. A unit is set up to gather facts and draw on experience. It has a direct pipeline to the boss but reports officially to a lesser light. Its direction comes through the pipeline, and its output goes back through the same channel. What a charade. The people in the unit run all over the company putting together dope on whatever subject the boss assigns. The boss uses the research to prove whatever point he wants to prove. Operating officers will find that some hasty remark they made will end up being used to lend strength to some high-level action the boss has taken.

Here's a couple of top management's best in the use of such wholly ghosting units. An office of corporate planning is a beaut. Out will come a directive giving every department head sixty days to come up with a five-year operating plan. The planning unit hashes over what comes in, and top management has enough ideas to back up anything it wants to do. Another dandy is a special body to control costs. Plans to control costs come in to this unit, while the padded budgets go to their regular places. The boss is thus on record for being extremely cost conscious but allowed to be the only man to see both the budgets and the plans to keep costs down. He can open the money spigot for his pet projects and turn off the funds for everything else. Top management has wholly ghosted in its most subtle way.

As an operating person, I have had my share of directives out of channels, requests for figures out of a clear blue sky, and high level looking papers signed by well-meaning people with little rank. I must admit that I never learned just how to handle these spooky kinds of things. I couldn't just ignore them; they came down that pipeline from the top. I often wondered how so many of my bosses could send fizz water down the pipeline and expect my blood back. Thank God that I got disgusted early with my own attempts to ghost; they gave me sympathy later for those I saw who felt the need to fake the birth of wisdom.

Management consultants are often used as ghosts. A friend of mine spent years working on a field training course for salesmen in his company. He did his job so well that his popularity became a threat to some of the men above him. Out of nowhere came a consultant who placed a recommendation on the desk of a man in top management that pointed toward some changes in the major training thrust. My friend got frightened and took his talent elsewhere—dumped in the name of the wholly ghost. I have to laugh now, but a consulting ghost was used on me. There was a cost-of-living increase across the board except for those of us in the executive officer ranks. There was no real reason for me to receive an increase, and I could not have been upset by not getting one, but out of left field came a full-page letter which presumed to tell me why no raise. I put a red line under these words,

We have just had a Personnel Consulting Firm evaluate all Executive Officers as to future potential and current earnings.

> They have made some recommendations in relationship to the age of the group, the current performance of the individuals, and their future worth to the company. We have taken their advice in arriving at raises for executives at this time.

Now I know that these words were not used in exactly this way, but the message flung itself at me. Having seen no one from that firm, I had been evaluated by some kind of ghost. Management had a perfect right to leave my pay where it was, but it took gall to use a ghost to tell me that I was either too old, too lousy, or too over-the-hill to get a boost. I would have been much happier if the gall to write that letter had been replaced by the guts to tell me where I stood face-to-face. Admittedly, management is under no obligation to do either. That's why it all seems so laughable now.

The coup de grace of wholly ghosting is putting a disembodied spirit in charge of a full-fledged operating department. A Mr. Big in top management sets up a ghost of his former self. Every big shot has carved out his reputation while the head of some department. He either breathed life into a dead horse or crested on top of a big wave. His timing was right, and he hit the heights at a very young age. He popped into the pearly gates of top corporate management basking in the glory of his departmental exploits, and he will never let go of that past scene of power. Until he retires, his old department will act as his pissing post and security blanket. He will put a ghost in charge to assure complete accord with everything he wants to do in his old stomping grounds. Come to think of it, it's better to be a ghost in such a spot. Hooray for ghosts! They can wrap themselves around their bosses in loving affection and be pissed on without getting wet.

Everybody knows when a ghost has been installed. They also know that Mr. Ghost will be in constant contact with God the Father; that whither thou goest, Big Shot, there will Mr. Ghost be also. Here's the type of guy that makes the best ghost. He is younger than the boss for sure. War horses are hard to push around. He's less brainy but looks bright. Spirits need not be burdened down with the smarts, but they must look good enough not to frighten people. He will share the boss's outside interests, or learn to in a hurry. If the boss likes to fish, he'll bait his hook. He is a big man, for the big boss wants a big shadow. Also, size will help the ghost when he tackles the other department heads on the boss's pet projects. He is not a tough guy in his own right, but he makes a good agent for the boss's own style of muscle bending. He will not be liked, but the boss doesn't want him to be. If he were liked, he might get the help of the outfit and become his own man. He could even threaten the boss's old departmental record. But if he's not liked, people will remember the good old days and keep their ties to the old guy longer. The man who installs a ghost has no plans to make him popular. Neither does he have plans to make him effective. Once a ghost, always a ghost, but herein lies the final problem for the boss with his ghost: the time will come when the ghost must go.

Take it from this old ghost-watcher. Ghosts live forever, and don't even age rapidly. They do not have to wrestle with tough decisions nor suffer worry pangs. Their bosses do so for them. Why shouldn't they live long lives? Like old soldiers, ghosts can only fade away, and they insist on fading away upward. I have seen a boss try to throw one down, but the ghost haunts the premises when such an attempt is made. Rather than stir up any more spooky venom around the joint, the top management guy prepares a higher place for the ghost who has worn thin back in that old department. Usually ghost number two takes over.

If money is no object, a company can maintain a stable of ghosts and often does, but the time will come when some ghosts have to be blown away. It's a tense time in the ivory tower when the breeze of departure starts blowing. In the crustiest of corporate bosses, there is some milk of sympathy and some degree of remorse in such situations. But when they have to, they muster up the courage to slip the ghost's name to a manpower relocation service and await developments. It's nice to know that your ghost is going to light somewhere with a high-paying job. All over America in big business, there is a collage of ghosts at large, sticking to the top dollar wherever they touch down. Being ghosts, they can't be buried. Every company has spawned its share of these spooks and must pay its part of the tab for their continuous upkeep. Being unable to kill them off, they swap them around. The ghosts of our corporate world are not the cause of mismanagement, they are the result of it. They have neither the strength nor the will to screw things up. The tough, self-oriented bosses with the iron hands and acid bottoms are the ones who goof. No need to beware of ghosts. Beware of the wholly ghosting business barons who create them. Let us pray.

5

REVERSE LAME DUCKING

HERBERT HOOVER DIDN'T have the happiest tour of duty as President of the United States, and he never heard the last of it. No matter what great service he rendered later, millions would never let him off the hook for being in the White House when the Great Depression got started. As a young teen-ager, I recall the grownups talking after November of 1932 about how bad it was that the country had to wait until March of the next year to see the last of Herbert. Everybody in my neck of the woods was sure that Franklin Delano Roosevelt was going to turn things around. I don't know whether or not you are an admirer of FDR, but it's a cinch that he had one of the easiest men to follow of all our presidents. Even this kid was anxious to see Hoover hit the road, and I was not surprised to see the Lame Duck Amendment to the Constitution passed in 1933. Poor Herbert Hoover wasn't even welcome as a lame duck.

Would you believe that Mr. Hoover's balcony appearances every four years at the National Republican Convention after television came along could cause me to lean toward the other party? I was always seeing the last of the lame duck presidents instead of the truly great humanitarian that he later became. One doesn't hear the term "lame duck" very often anymore, for it is usually used in connection with elected officials. Since 1933, we have been moving the beaten out of the picture quickly to make room for the newly elected, but we really shouldn't let the handle die. There are too many lame ducks in other pursuits to give up the description, and big business has its share. I followed several in my day and, going into retirement, I was one.

Roosevelt was lucky to follow a loser and really couldn't go anywhere but up. He started by closing the banks in the whole damn country as his first step in becoming a hero. That's like closing the schools as the first step in a program to better education. Things were so bad in the economy that the very tool of recovery, commercial banking, had to be shut down to keep a panicking people from draining off the supply of money. The point is that some men arrive on the scene when things are so dead that success is not hard to come by. History is full of such people. Take your choice from the man who followed Nero, to Ulysses S. Grant, who took over the Union army after a series of stupid generals, and got on with winning the Civil War. Many men in big business management fall into just such pitiful situations and come out looking like the real thing by the grace of their forerunner's utter failure. The most appreciated leadership I ever spread around was more due to the hate lying all over the place for the guy who left than to my own doing.

I like to come in behind a weak stick to take over his mess. It's like being a bright new rug on a dirty floor. People see you and are prone to take your ideas in a hurry—and so it is with following a lame duck. No matter how strong he once was, there is usually a slacking off in his own efforts as his end draws near, not to mention the slowing down of the total unit as it waits for him to leave. Even when the guy going out keeps on pushing himself to the very last, the people under him are always waiting around. He is doomed to be a lame duck, no matter how hard he tries not to be. No departing leader's outfit will let him get away without turning him into some kind of excuse for what might go wrong in the immediate future. It's just not good sense to miss the chance to cover one's self against any harm that could rear its ugly head within days after the old guy has left.

But even this situation is not the worst part of the lame duck matter. The real wounds to a company are caused by the "reverse lame duckers," those who by design cut back on the all-out pursuit of progress while waiting for the top man to move on. These people are the heirs to the jobs being vacated by the retiring men. And don't forget, there are always a series of promotions to come out of any man's departure. Three or four levels of management usually freeze when a high-up guy is going out. Each in turn is waiting for his new piece of the pie. The company would be lucky if all they did was wait, but it's not just a matter of going into second gear. Unless a man is exceptionally devoted to consistent effort and has the guts of a levee mule to walk by troubled waters, he will give in to temptation in two ways. I wish I could report my own godliness in resisting these two cesspools of human conduct, but I can't.

Once in the line of succession, one can only lose by taking a chance on some new project. When I was set to move up in rank, I would shy away from risky business like the plague. I never knew a man who looked for big or costly new developments when he thought he had a jump in title coming up as the result of a lame duck's moving on. The risk is too great. Isn't it ironic that guts are so needed in big business and yet one doesn't dare use his in many situations for fear that doing so will backfire? Is there any wonder that cautious cowards can steadily rise to jobs where backbone is needed? No, it's easy to see how they do, but this point is still not the greatest curse of reverse lame ducking. So what's worse? Hold your nose, I'll tell you: it is the careful storing of good ideas by a man expecting promotion until he gets his new spot. When one starts this process, everything of value oozing up from below gets stockpiled, to be dusted off at a more fitting time—a time selected for its favorable odds to make the hoarder look smart. Being able to go into a new job with a stable of new ideas gives a man a look of brilliance that he really doesn't have. Looming upon the scene with quick changes that work can never hurt anybody and can set one up for instant respect by those who do not know the bright ideas were saved up over a period of time. Oh sure, the guys who put the ideas in the pot in the first place will hate his guts, but who's dumb enough to go running around claiming the boss's new idea as his own? Nobody! The reverse lame ducker has avoided risk and bolstered up his brain in one motion.

Let's take a look at one flock of ducks, some lame, some flying backwards. The time is December 1970. There were six men at or above the senior V.P. rank at the end of 1968, but here's the lineup going into 1971:

Chairman, Chief Executive Officer	Age 63
President	Age 63
Executive V.P.-heir apparent	Age 51
Executive V.P.	Age 61
Executive V.P.	Age 48
Senior V.P.	Age 45
Senior V.P.	Age 46
Senior V.P.	Age 40

Five, six, pick up sticks. Seven, eight, lay them straight. Five, six, look for fame. Seven, eight, pull up lame. Five, six, time will pass. Seven, eight, run out of gas.

The chairman has been the main decision-maker since 1949 and is close to being the most respected man in his industry. There is no way that he is going to personally slow down. It's not an easy thing to turn him into a lame duck, but there are some pretty tough cookies who are willing to try. He has a sales background and has spent much of his time keeping in touch with that department. However, he has a grip on the rest of the company except for the investment guy, the executive V.P., age 61.

The president is the chairman's alter ego and grew up as controller. He is extremely active in diversification and new ventures. He might lame duck in some things, but nobody is likely to slow down his desire to add a quick new layer of something to this old-line life insurance company. And time is running out on both him and the chairman.

The heir apparent is also from sales, for the chairman wants to continue that background at the top of the outfit. He sold himself short as part of the price he had to pay to get in line for the top, but people don't hold this fact against him. Two years look like eternity to him, but he has no choice; he must wait. He's in charge of all departments that work directly with the field and has the greatest chance to screw up by far.

The 61-year-old is the only one, besides the chairman, who can go to the bathroom on his own initiative, which he does often, sometimes spattering other parts of the company in the process; there's nothing mean about it—he's just a hard-driving man with the well-being of his own troops utmost in mind. There will be no lame ducking in his area, nor any reverse lame ducking either. The investment job will get done right up to snuff on a day-to-day basis. Deals for dollars can't be saved up.

The other executive V.P., age 48, is a lawyer and is working on governmental relations, with some internal chores. His chance to goof is almost nil, and his fate is riding more on what the heir apparent might do to lose the ball game than on what he might do himself to win it. The chairman has put it on the grapevine that this man is one of three possible choices to take over the company. This gossip shakes up the heir apparent, but doesn't fool many people down the line.

The 45-year-old senior V.P. is in charge of sales and is a ghost beyond recall. However, the chairman has given him more social time than he has given any other man, and the rest of the crowd cannot afford to write him off completely. He expects to float upward in some manner, but doesn't know how badly the heir apparent wants to side-track him for good.

The senior V.P. at 46 is the third man the chairman has said is man enough to take over. After being rather unknown for years, he has moved up very fast in the last six or seven to arrive at a rank that few would have ever considered possible. The chairman has sealed a deal with the heir apparent that this man will move right along. In fact, the chairman will see to it himself. He has little to gain or lose personally, but you can bet your bottom dollar that he will blow with the wind of the heir apparent until the smoke dies down.

The young senior V.P. is aware that he's had it for the moment, but even he knows he's got it good. Being from a technical background, far removed from sales, he would like to see the influence of the sales side of the house cut back. However, he can see that it won't be, and is worried about where the ghost may light. One thing he knows for sure is that the cost picture in the company is not likely to get too much attention over the next two years, and this point bothers him. The top guys going out won't go down in history for having cut costs; to make their final mark, they have to spend money, which suits the heir apparent, for the higher the unit costs when he takes over, the more chance he'll have to keep on spending.

I am a 53-year-old, who has already worked out a retirement package for himself with the heir apparent. You can take your choice in how you look at me. I can either be a guy who really wants to get off the team and see what he can do on his own strength, or I can be a lame duck, walking around outside the pen, throwing sour grapes over the fence. Take your choice. In any event, I have two years to spend trying not to impede progress. That was easy, I just got out of the mainstream, completely away from any area in which

I had previously had a voice. My successor didn't have to save up a single idea. He had the job already.

What do you think? Will the two top dogs go lame? Will the heir apparent continue to save up ideas, which he's been doing for two years already? Will the other candidates for the top take the chairman seriously and shoot the moon in an effort to jump over the man with the inside track? Will the president get to make a big move in the new venture area and go out famous for something after all those years of dog-robbing for the chairman? I'll give you a few specifics and let you draw your own conclusions.

There was no slacking off in the energy put forth by the two top guys, but new products were hard to come by, and new programs to push sales didn't show up. It got easier and easier for the top management team to work like beavers on long-range matters and to ignore the immediate. There were smoke screens about cost control and increased productivity, but no real steps were taken. Enough hours went into the development of a five-year corporate plan to have paved Broadway from Forty-second Street to Columbus Circle, if the people had been working with concrete instead of sky pie. If this kind of stuff made lame ducks out of the two top guys, then that was their fate.

Before the time in question, I had the following experience with the heir apparent. Ten years earlier, he had the job that I had had in 1969. He had greatly sought a particular improvement in one part of the salesman's duties which had to do with getting paid certain fees. He had tried hard to get rid of a stupid requirement that shackled the field men, complicating their collection of this money. But every attempt he made to convince the other departments had gone astray. Now that he was executive V.P., he had the power to approve the move, if somebody could get the departments to sign off in favor of the change. I walked it through and presented it to him on a silver platter. It went into his storehouse of things to do at a more timely moment, like when he takes over. He'll need some meat to make instant hero sandwiches to feed the field. Do you think that this was the only morsel tucked away?

The other two front runners had a big chunk of the future safely salted down. If either made an end run and failed, he could lose everything. The odds were great that they would sit still. No, the time for risk taking was past. Kicking up their heels was about as likely as Spiro Agnew trying to do Nixon out of the Republican nomination for president in 1972. I will leave it up to you as to whether or not their desire for safety would rob them of their courage to stand up to the day-to-day demands for action that every man in high places must face. One thing I know, they won't fly anything alone. The heir apparent will be in the picture on everything. If he wants to move, well and good. If he wants to drag his feet or save an idea, they'll help him do that too.

The president got his new venture; the company bought another life insurance company for fifty-five million dollars. No doubt, the risk made sense in dollars and cents. Time will tell if the move was really good for the company, but it's a study in reverse lame ducking to look at what took place. The chairman and the president decided to buy the company, but they got cold feet on taking the bull by the horns. So they called a meeting of the eight guys we're talking about and put the proposition forward. Then they got up and walked out of the room, saying, "We will not be around much anymore; you men should decide this without us." They made lame ducks out of themselves. Mr. Heir Apparent had something he couldn't save. The company was bought; can you imagine the guy having the guts to say no in that spot? It took no guts to say yes, for if things go wrong, the blame can be laid on the dear departed. Not only that, the departed can point to the record and say that they were out of the room when the decision to buy was made. Let's hope that things go right, but if they don't, it will be hard to say who really did buy that company.

This process is not confined to the top side of any corporation. All up and down the line, it goes on. But no matter the level, it is not the lame ducks that hurt a company, it's the Wongo Wongo birds, who fly backwards to keep their tails safe from threats to the rear, that cause an outfit to lose its way when leadership is on its way out. Reverse lame ducking is for the birds, but it should be saved for birds of prey, not little lame ducks limping away. Lame ducks would rather die than hurt a company. Why can't the people coming along behind them keep going all out pending their departure? If I could have done it, I wouldn't need to ask you that question.

6

NIPPLETISM

WHEN A MAN gets a base of power, he becomes frustrated by his personal limitations with regard to its use. He has only two arms, two legs, two eyes, and two ears. He can be in only one place at any one time, and he is confined to what he can see, hear, and do, wherever he is; and being in charge of something does not give him complete power over the people involved with it. So what chance does a department head in a big company have to know even a fraction of what's going on at every point in time in his whole area? For sure, the head guy in any outfit knows but little about the total picture. No wonder big shots in big business get frustrated by their feelings of being out of touch with day-to-day matters. No man in such a spot can resist the urge to add some legs, arms, eyes, and ears to his own.

The army is so aware of this crying personal need that it gives generals an aide-de-camp. The spot calls for a man of low rank, for he will not need power of his own. The general will turn his power over to the aide, who is most always a young man. The younger he is, the faster he can move around to see, hear, and dig up the things the general wants to know about. It's not unusual for him to have a marker on his vehicle to make him stick out as the general's helper. When he rides up, colonels bow down. They see stars in his bars and behave as though the old man himself were right there. The general has indeed increased the number of places he can be at any one time. The more he can keep the young officer flitting about over the command, the more real the general's feeling of power becomes.

Big businessmen now have equivalent aides. Assistants to the president are showing up regularly, and the same effect can be pulled off under a variety of job titles. No matter what the steps taken, the point is that business big shots are just as starved as military big shots for the extra sense of strength that mobile flunkies seem to give them. But the cost of this activity is great, making it unlikely that any manager below the very top can come up with such a man. So some informal method has to be used, making it necessary to stake out such eyes and ears and legs among the young men who have other duties, but who are willing to carry out the role of snoop for the boss. It's not easy to set up the system. No manager can bring it out into the open and have an announcement made that young Mr. Smith is hereby given the extra duty of "spying" for the boss. If the boss had a son in the outfit, junior could perform the role without people getting too upset. They would just face the matter and take measures to see that they didn't get caught in a crossfire between father and son. But if you don't know who might be one of these guys, your conduct becomes rather self-protecting. Nepotism is nowhere near the threat in this regard that "nippletism" is.

Nippletism is the adoption of a fair-haired boy by a big shot, with a father-son-like deal in mind. No birth certificate is required and no announcement of little feet running around the house has to be made. Strong men like to baby something and get a big kick out of putting their power behind someone in a lesser spot. Couple this urge with the need for extra legs, and arms and eyes and ears, and few managers can resist adopting at least one young guy. As I moved up in rank, the temptation to do so got stronger and stronger. I did it once, only to find that I lost interest in it forever. My baby fed on me so constantly that I began to wish I had a pouch to put him in. Needless to say, my nipple got sore, and the weaning came quickly. Back to this later, but such bonds do go on for years in some cases. There will always be bosses offering themselves up as fathers and young men willing to stake their futures on being adopted.

While I never sat in the top spot of the total company, I did have charge of a part with over a thousand people in it—not exactly a small base of power. That's when I learned that sitting there in that catbird seat is no bed of roses. Underneath me, there were people who had every reason to think that they were more right for my job than I was. Countless functions were being carried out that I did not know how to do myself. The sheer number of things going on could almost make me panic. The fear of not knowing which walls might be tumbling down was stifling. I began to see that a seat of power put one out of touch with what was going on and that having power could strip one of the feeling of safety that routine work provides. The higher I went, the more I became aware of how little control I had, and the more starved I got for some kind of bond with some people below. Having the entire unit at my beck and call was one thing, but it gave me no warm feeling, like close contact and intimate knowledge could have brought. To say that I wanted to be loved would be an overstatement, but I did wish for someone to feed on me. Hard nosed guys are not incapable of growing nipples; when they do, they have to adopt sons.

Nepotism is not outlawed in many businesses merely because the son acts as an automatic snooper for his old man. It's outlawed because the father favors the son with title and money, far beyond his earned rewards. Blood is thicker than water, and as the old saying goes, "If your relatives won't help you, who the hell will?" Sons do have a way of shooting upward through a company like a rocket, when their fathers hold big jobs topside. Nippletism leads to the same thing. Adopted sons rise like cream through milk, if they please their fathers. How do they please them? First, by loving them up. Second, by deserting all others. Finally, by acting as their extra legs, arms, and so on.

My move to adopt a corporate son started out innocently enough. I thought my only motive was the need to have something going with at least one man out of which could come a relationship of personal worth, not just business dealings. Golf games, weekend trips with wives, and other strictly side issues were the beginning. But, outside of business, we had about as much in common as a bull moose and a nanny goat. So what pulled us together? My need for another set of legs, arms, eyes, and ears—plus his desire to vault ahead by tying on to my coattail. The mind is fantastic. It can take a very lousy desire and dress it up to look like a most worthwhile cause. I didn't really want to father that young guy for any reason other than to use him. He didn't put himself at my disposal except to further his own purposes. Overnight, he was snooping for me, and I was lining up his rewards at the expense of other people. When I caught myself about to give him a raise out of all proportion to other men in his grade, I turned my back on nippletism forever. Thank goodness that I nipped it in the bud, before the guy got hurt.

Having had this experience, I couldn't really resent other high-level managers who played the same game. However, I surely didn't want to get caught like a fly in some trap the two men might lay, so I kept my eyes open for sprouting nipples and hungry babies. They are always there but not always visible. I learned to watch the foursomes at the company golf tournament and to keep an ear out for who went fishing with whom. In this way, I came up with early warning signs, but sooner or later, father-son roles come out into the open. When one does, it usually means that both parties have decided to live with the deal, regardless of where it may lead them. Knowing this fact, and being afraid to buck the high-up guy, most people just grunt and try to keep from getting caught in a crossfire. As for me, I felt the need to muddy the water for the pair to some extent, at least to let them know that I wasn't blind.

Here's how I did it. I took the baby into my "overconfidence." I told him everything I planned to do plus a whole lot more. He had no way of picking out the wheat from the chaff. I was careful to include a batch of things that I knew the old man hated. It was easy to recall the things that the boss had thrown out years earlier and to trot them by him again by telling the baby how much confidence I had in them now. The baby hadn't been around long enough to know about the top guy's dislikes. I could even do a snow job on the young man and send him to the boss's office really excited about some china egg from long ago. As a kid, I used to catch the neighbor's dog in the family garden, tie two or three tin cans to his tail, and send him home rattling and running. Duping the baby was a version of the same game, and sometimes, it kept the guy out of my hair as it often kept the dog at home. At least it made him run when he saw me coming. The end result of this baiting would be the boss's lowered confidence in the young man. He was shocked at the lack of common sense shown by the young guy's interest in these china eggs. Of course, he'd call me to see if I really had them back in mind. I'd say, "Hell no! Who told you so?" He couldn't even answer, for fear that his baby would get in trouble. Make you want to laugh? When I tell you that I, the boss, and the baby were making over $100,000 a year among us, you'll want to cry.

Adopted sons are willing to take much abuse, for the prizes are enormous. While a real father will exercise some restraint in what he does for junior, nippletism can blind a boss to the ills growing out of the adoption and cause him to push the baby much more than he would have pushed his own flesh and blood. This is particularly so when he starts getting some flack from other people about what he is doing.

I would never bitch to the boss about his baby, for it would only make him mad and cause him to throw his weight around all the more. That's why I had to use the tin can method. No boss likes to have his power challenged, and that's what one does if one gripes about the baby. Knowing this human trait, adopted sons go out of their way to drum up abuse.

I know one who took on the whole law division of his company and picked a huge fight over a matter that the big boss should never have had to get in on. It should have been dealt with at the subdepartmental level, but the young guy salted a small open sore and bred an infection that couldn't even be resolved at the department head rank. He made sure that his father in the corporate heaven of the top executive suite had to back him up. Father did, too, and a fine lawyer, who was really right, was sidetracked in his career. There is no doubt in my mind that the adopted son caused the rift by design, not chance, and that he knew in advance how the thing was going to come out. Otherwise, he would never have forced the issue. Adopted sons learn early not to suck on a dry nipple. This situation taught me not to try to take candy away from corporate babies who have extremely loyal fathers; such an attempt is a good way to lose your ass and all its fixtures.

What happens to these young guys? One of two things. Some get carried away with their transferred power and put the boss in over his head. (If this situation takes place to the top guy's discomfort, he will just break off the adoption and leave the baby to his own devices. The rest of the people perceive this break quickly, and there is no hell like that experienced by an abandoned corporate baby. Most leave the company.) But usually the young man is too smart to put his boss out on a limb, and he survives to get his hands on a big job. He's more than likely a vice president before he is forty, but you can be sure that he has but one friend at court. Everybody below him hates his guts, and those above, between him and his father, keep their aluminum athletic supporters on. But once the top dog gets the guy up to the vice president's level, Mr. Big tends to think that his obligation is discharged. If he does feel that way, he will turn his adopted son into a ghost, keep him around for a couple of years, and then float him away to another company. The senior V.P. ghost in the previous chapter was dealt with exactly in this way. Before the heir apparent could take over, he was gone. The cycle was complete: nourished by nippletism, matured as wholly-a-ghost, and blown away to the boondocks. One can make a raft of money this way. Want some?

7

HO! HO! HO! DOWNING

THE EXTREMES OF human emotion are wrapped up in ho! ho! ho! Coming from Santa Claus, it lights up faces and fills us with hope. Coming from one's boss, it can put a scowl on your face and turn your dreams of business success to ashes. Coming from a circus clown, it puts laughter into hearts and stirs up mirth in young and old alike. Coming from business big shots, it can put people down and dampen the spirits of valuable men and women. A hoedown is a community dancing party with hillbilly music, to which folks flock to shake a leg and to find self-expression. A "ho! ho! ho! down" is a boss's one-man laugh fest that makes one of his key people feel like a hillbilly and causes him to refrain from doing his own thing. Such laughter, in effect, says to that man, "How can you be so stupid?"

Hillbillies have an innate sense of knowing what to stay away from, and big business does not have to cope with many unpolished rural diamonds. Moonshine in the stills is far more likely to be big in a rube's life than monkeyshines in the carpeted halls of industry. Such people take to the hills and enjoy the hoedowns of their own kind, thus avoiding the ho! ho! ho! downing they would face if they showed up at the door of some company full of men who put a great deal of stock in looks. Retreating to one's own kind, as the hillbilly does, can shield a man from many of the hurts that men have a way of inflicting on one another. But even in a company where the guys behind the desks look like carbon copies of each other, many people get laughed at and have their ideas singed by the hot breath of scoffing bosses. I have been on both ends of this sick game, crawling away under laughter from above, yet heehawing mightily as a body from below tried to get some new thing started, which I didn't quite dig.

Bosses can laugh some of a company's best idea material right out of existence. If a person's pet concept of a new way to do an old job has been guffawed away by a high-up man, it is unlikely that he will bring it up again. Not only that, he will probably not suggest anything else that might earn him laughter. For every man with the guts to face the laughter that can come from old-fashioned bosses, there are dozens who just will not risk it. As General Billy Mitchell found out after World War I, the men in charge are not always ready for new ideas. He had the gall to state that an airplane could sink a battleship, and crusty old navy men said he was crazy as they ho! ho! ho! downed him out of the hearing rooms of that day. And the army to which he belonged didn't help him, for the old horse soldiers in high spots weren't even ready for the tank, let alone the bombing plane. As he met more and more ridicule, Billy Mitchell found out that it's hard to laugh alone when the world laughs at you.

To escape the whole messy scene, all he had to do was to crawl away and let time set a new stage more favorable to his ideas, but Mitchell wasn't built that way; he had the guts to keep right on saying that a flying machine could sink a battleship, as he plodded down the road to personal disgrace. Few men in corporate life would show such courage. Now I wouldn't want to give you the impression that many business matters are played for quite as high stakes as those for which Mitchell was playing, what with Adolf Hitler, Tojo, and all, but the truth is that some young corporate tigers do come up with very worthy projects and see them go down the drain to the music of "Ho! Ho! Ho!, That Won't Go." Most crawl away and wait, rather than take the chance of being branded as a troublemaker. One thing is certain. If a man goes under to the degree that he has to quit, he will never make a move of value to that company. So some flirt with danger, but do not push anything hard enough to become threatened by it. Survival at least leaves them on the scene, where some of their ideas may prove acceptable. General Mitchell happened to believe that the strength of the free world was at stake, and he was willing to go out of existence as a producing person to keep the spotlight on the issue.

Talking about myself in the same breath with a man of such raw courage is the height of something—egotism, I guess—but the reader is more likely to be like me than like the general. In fact, you may have already had your test under fire of ho! ho! ho! downing in your company. If so, you'll see the point of these two little examples clearly. When I first came charging into the home office from the front line, field sales, I was determined to come up with a new financing plan for beginning life insurance men. I had been around the horn with the ones in use, both as a new man and as a field manager trying to get men started in the business. Rather than expose my thoughts too early, I did six months of research to check on the reactions of other managers in the field to my basic thought. After finding out that they liked the idea, I decided that the time was right to unveil my little beauty. I can still wake up in the middle of the night and find myself cringing under the strains of derisive laughter. Even after the thing had been killed for the moment, one big shot laughed it up again in a full-fledged executive officers' meeting just to make sure the chairman heard about it. I was low enough to look up at a snake, but the guy had really made me mad. That's when I decided that I would roll up my sleeves again. Would you believe that it took seven years to overcome the bad effects of the initial ho! ho! ho!? Would you believe that the idea saved the company a half million bucks a year while making the field happy, after it finally got used?

About three years before retirement started to look good to me, I stumbled upon a young idea in this old body. It had to do with counting new business before the policies were actually written, so that agencies could receive credit for business without having to drive the underwriting department wild to issue the policies. I saw the move as a great way to have peace in the family without giving a lot of money away. The laughter from the control side of the house was bad enough, but the former salesmen in top management were not in any less of a mood to ho! ho! ho! I was so excited about having such a youthful thought that caution didn't enter my head. I decided to go all out then for what could be my last really innovative idea. People at my salary level were not supposed to seek changes that would expose them to ho! ho! ho! Not only that, they were not expected to play around with such sacred things as business credit. In any event, I made myself so active in the pursuit of this idea that it was done. The laughter was upstaged by my don't-give-a-damn attitude. But I am convinced that it took so much out of this old mind and body, that creeping off to rest started to look attractive. Did it bring peace in the family? Yes it did, and I consider it well worth what it took out of me.

Would you believe that these two things make up the entire list of major creative changes that I was able to bring about in my whole career—one every decade? Would you believe that I am probably far ahead of the average man and that ho! ho! ho! limits the chances that anyone has to bring about change? Just seeing somebody else get the laughter treatment is enough to make most men keep still. When Billy Mitchell was put down for pounding on the importance of air power, no one could tell how many other men went underground with their thoughts about how to better prepare for national defense. Companies never know either what the overall toll of ho! ho! ho! downing is, but the fact is that many men do keep their best thinking to themselves for fear of being laughed at.

In the world of now, big business is at a sort of crossroads about the looks of the people it will allow within its walls. At the clerical level, it has already had to get off its kick about appearance. As skirts go up and down, bras go on and off, pants wax and wane, hair brushes rise and fall, and shoes go flat, the image makers have to give up. Whether or not the girls are big on women's lib, they do have a strong desire to follow their own noses when it comes to dress. If the companies want the typewriters beat upon, they have to give up some of their old thoughts on looks. The girls were smart. They broke the barriers with the miniskirt. Men are not likely to cling to tradition when the view from the desk is so improved, and the mini didn't take long to catch on. But that got the cat-of-appearances out of the bag and laid the companies open to further change. Having sat still for the mini, they could hardly clamp down on the long pants which took away all the fringe benefits of the short skirts. The end result is that most companies now have some kind of rule which says that neatness is all-important, but that at the clerical level one can choose one's own style of dress.

At the management level, however, image still plays a strong role. Ho! ho! ho! downing for looks alone is not yet out of corporate life. In the past, the personnel department did the laughing for the whole outfit, and it merely turned away the job seekers who didn't look the part. But now the guys and gals coming in to see about work are coming off campuses where jeans are formal wear, full beards are commonplace, and hair styles for boys and girls are hard to tell apart. Underneath those nonconforming exteriors are the minds of tomorrow, and they better not be laughed away. So the personnel guys have to look below the surface to find the gems of manhood that the companies need, and they have to send them on to the operating departments for final judgment. They must be careful not to laugh them away for looks alone.

The difference between these people and the hillbillies is very clear. Rather than shy away from a person or a company that would be prone to laugh at them, this new breed is more likely to force themselves on the man or the institution that would try to put them down by laughter. Having been born into the marching, shouting, banner-bearing generation, they will picket you before they will shrink before your ridicule. Big business will have to take them about as they are, as far as looks are concerned. Ho! ho! ho! downing must be a thing of the past on dress, hair style, and beards, if a company is to get the brains it needs. I predict that business will make this adjustment, but it will never be able to get completely away from putting down ideas through dumb laughing. I also predict that many of this new breed will be very reluctant to hide from their laughing bosses and that the quitting rate among them will be very high as they look for fields in which ideas are nourished rather than scoffed at.

So much for the serious side of ho! ho! ho! downing. It also has its comical side. When two or more big shots start chasing the same promotion, they are very prone to try to laugh each other down. When a person is threatened by anything, he has three choices as far as his outward show of emotion is concerned. He can laugh, cry, or stand frozen like the Sphinx. Crying is not in the cards for a big businessman, and standing like the Sphinx is a sign of not being able to cope—a dead giveaway of weakness. That leaves only laughter. At the mention of the competition's name, every wary hot shot looking for quick promotion will ho! ho! ho! I remember so many times saying something like this, "Ho! ho! ho!, have you heard about old Joe's latest brainstorm?" Or this, "Heehaw, didn't Joe act stupid at the meeting the other day when the big boss cut him off short?" These are only matched in meanness and crassness by the things that Joe was doing and saying to point ridicule at me. It's a wonder that both men in such situations don't get blown away. They would, if the guys picking between them were not a product of the same process and still willing to play the same game themselves.

If you haven't seen this type of thing turned into a road show, you have missed a treat. When really big promotions are coming up for grabs, the various candidates are often making speeches all around the country at meetings or conventions. There is no way that men in such spots are going to give up the chance to laugh at their opposition. Many times, they will be showing up on the same platform, and the audience will get a double shot of such behavior. You'll hear bad jokes about silly people, into which the listeners are supposed to slip the name of the man being laughed at. You'll see baiting of one man by another to trap him into some kind of reaction designed to make him cause laughter at himself, and you would be amazed at how many times the trap works. You'll see the top boss add to the excitement by making a pass at one or both parties involved, thereby telling all people that he alone is going to be the final judge of the amateur contest now being put on for their amusement. There will be no phone numbers or post office boxes given out to let the audience vote; Mr. Big will make the selection, if he hasn't already. It's cheap entertainment, and ends up cheapening the men involved, but they will do it to themselves every time.

Since one can never head off another's ho! ho! ho!, the only defense against derisive laughter is not to lose one's composure. Watch any stand-up, night club comedian and you will see his uneasiness when the audience does not laugh and instead sits in silence. Any joke-teller prefers a boo to utter silence, for even a boo can serve as the springboard to another joke. If you become the victim of ho! ho! ho!, from either a narrow-minded boss or a venomous competitor for a promotion, your stock is most likely to rise if you refuse to fight fire with fire. However, on each such occasion, you will be forced to decide whether or not you can afford the time to extinguish the opposing blaze.

Within the scope of ho! ho! ho!, human emotions swing to and fro. The bigger the business, the more childish the games can become. Bobbing for apples can bring out the laughs, but so can grab bags for big jobs, or pick-up-sticks in the game of corporate life. Nobody wins from laughing off his playmates; one of them may come up with the biggest stick, in which case, he'll want to play a game called "watch your ass." I suggest that he watch his own tail; help the company by setting up an atmosphere that will bring out the best ideas of all people, young and old, big and little; and keep ho! ho! ho! downing to a minimum.

8

UPPER LEVELING

BEING POWERLESS TO make many large improvements in everlasting corporate life with his own unique mind, most men in big companies try to get some small part of their thinking into the large projects and programs being considered by their department heads. Nothing of any real worth is likely to happen unless the top man does see the proposed move as good for the total unit. Many men who make the final decisions know that new steps to make things better are most often brought about by taking fragments of thoughts from several people and blending them into an idea more acceptable than any single concept from any single mind. Such leaders set up processes to encourage all members to put their two cents in, so to speak, and people usually do. Many new and improved changes can come in this way, but few individuals ever get the ultimate personal thrill that comes from being the recognized father of some really unique and profitable new wrinkle.

A little piece of "me," a little piece of "thee," and little bits of another "three" can make up some kind of mixture called "we." For my money, this process is the most degrading part of corporate existence, but just try to stay alive any other way. To stay alive, people look for ways to get little pieces of themselves into the mainstream of departmental thinking and seldom go all out for anything they believe.

Knowing that their thoughts are going to be sifted before any part is put to use, they tend to do the first sifting themselves, in an effort to find a little piece of thinking most likely to fit into some larger patchwork quilt. Once they decide what that little piece is, they face the problem of how to get it into the idea kitty from which the final design of the new brainchild will come. No small part of the challenge is their boss, along with all the other bosses all the way to the guy on top.

Because so many of my bosses would pigeonhole ideas coming up from below, I had to find ways to float my thoughts and concepts around them. The best medium I found was hot air. I have an unlimited ability to generate it, and it is easily held together in a thin-skinned balloon. Sending up trial balloons became a way of life. When I had a boss who kept my ideas under his hat or had the habit of one day claiming them as his own, I would blow up a balloon, stuff in some of my notions, and waft it by him into the hands of someone higher up. I might or might not give him a smell of the contents. I was "upper leveling" my ideas to avoid having them sidetracked or picked off by my boss. He, of course, had to protect himself to avoid giving his boss the impression that he didn't know what I was doing. Once he got torpedoed from above by one of my ideas that should have come to him from below, he had to work out a way to stay out of such boxes.

All he had to do was pass my ideas on up, and I would not balloon him. He did not have to indorse them or lend his support in any way; I just did not want him to stifle them. But few men will take this direct approach to stop upper leveling. They do not want to stop doing it to their own bosses and, therefore, are prone to put up with it from below. I don't recall any attempts to keep me from sending up trial balloons. In the first place, it is easy to fake knowing about whatever the bigger boss has found in a balloon. If a guy over me asks about some thought drifting up from below my level, all I have to do is say, "I haven't checked that out with Jim today. Give me a couple of minutes, and I'll call you back." In two minutes, I can become an authority on Jim's pet idea and can call back looking like an all-wise executive. I have been upper leveled by some pretty smart cookies, but no boss of mine ever knew it. It's easy to hide one's not knowing, so bosses seldom take tough steps to stop the practice. In the second place, it is also easy to get a boss's reaction to an idea, without knowing what it is yourself. All one has to do is add these words to the delaying tactics above: "By the way, what did you think of the deal?" If the guy says he likes it, you know how interested to become yourself. So you end the call like this: "I think it has merit, too, be back to you in a few minutes." Then you run for Jim and get smart about his concept.

As you can see, upper leveling is not much of a drag, nor are trial balloons very destructive. In fact, one could look upon them as positive steps to make good things happen. In themselves, they do little damage; it's the conditions that foster them that cripple the thought power of big companies and cause men to resort to such clowning just to get heard. I soon learned that studying something, becoming an expert on it, researching to find new and simple steps to improve it, and writing up a recommendation to my boss were nowhere near enough to make certain that fast action would be taken on the matter. Coupled with this slowness in giving serious attention to anything, there is also the relationship side of creative thinking. Bosses see themselves threatened by too much innovative thinking on the part of any one man under them. I surely didn't want a man reporting to me to make me look badly in the smarts department, and nothing recommended from below ever got passed on up the line without my making an attempt to look as if I was part of the brain power behind the deal. No wonder that smart people tried to upper level me.

Most companies are so aware of both the pigeonholing of ideas by slow-moving bosses and the insecurity in those same bosses generated by the brains of certain people below them, that they often set up formal methods of upper leveling. Methods range from having a "suggestion box" to creating a full vice presidency for corporate projects. People are encouraged to drop their ideas into the box, or to get in touch with the vice president whose sole duty is to give top level consideration to new thinking. It is hoped that the log jam on thought power will be broken and that the company will come into possession of ideas that never would have surfaced under normal conditions. Happily, such surfacing is sometimes the result, but no more than a fraction of the brain power available is ever tapped. Here's why. If I don't put any ideas into the corporate bin for new developments, I can avoid having to fight for their adoption. Not only that, I can keep from having to sweat out their success or failure. While I may give great lip service to hating the little piece of "me," little piece of "thee" system, the fact is that I will not bare my ass to the fickle winds of adversity and lay myself open to being canned for having staked my reputation on a sour idea. Is there any way for the company to find out that it has a coward on its hands? No, for no one really expects each man to come up with original thinking. Ideas kept to one's self can never be discovered. Since nothing was expected, nothing has to be forthcoming, and any man can spend his career making no impact on the method of doing business. He will not get fired for lack of ideas, and he will make a good living just carrying out assigned duties. And don't get the notion that such a man is slated for low-level jobs. It's not necessarily so; some end up running the place.

When such a guy does take charge, he encourages upper leveling for his own selfish reasons. Not being able to generate much new thinking from his own head, he sets a tone around the company which breeds the practice. He'll call guys far down the line and fish for their thoughts. He'll be seen sitting with some middle management man with whom he can have no conceivable direct need to talk. He'll have lunch with some smart young thing under the guise of building morale, but he will be picking brains, not boosting spirits unless there is a martini in sight. Once this tone is set, you'll see as many balloons as there are around the opening of a new neighborhood gasoline station. People at all ranks will be dusting off their wind-making machines to fill up the balloons, and bosses will be polishing up their abilities to act bright about things they haven't even heard about. The balloons will float up and down, and each boss they pass will be trying to suck out a little air without puncturing any balloons. In this kind of atmosphere, it is easy for top management to pluck ideas from these balloons and send them back down the command ladder as if they were inspired of God and hand delivered by an angel to the top of the company. Many a man has sent an idea up and gotten it back unconnected with his name.

Since top management speaks for the company, and the company rightfully owns all ideas coming from its people, many men on top do not hesitate to take a piece of "me," a piece of "thee," and bits of many more to author changes under their own names. I say again that "me" and "thee" will never get the thrill that comes from recognition as the father of some truly unique new company wrinkle when management makes a habit of lifting all the goodies off the trial balloons to put out under its own labels. Have you ever given your boss a fairly good idea, only to meet some guy in the law department at lunch and have him say that he's checking something out for management that differs from your idea in just one respect—your name has been lost in the shuffle? If you haven't, let me give you a preview of your choices when first it happens to you. One, you can head for your boss and have it out with him for upper leveling your idea. He will swear that he gave you credit for it and will express his amazement that Mr. Big didn't play up your part in its birth. Two, you can go to the top guy and try to stake out a claim on your own idea. He'll tell you how long he's been thinking of this and pat you on the back for being so astute, but it will still belong to him.

Now I know that all of us good company-minded men, interested in progress, should not care about who gets credit for what. I also know that we should stop clowning around with the brain power in the outfit and get on with the job of developing new products and new methods of doing things, but I was never so selfless that I could push my personal position completely aside and give up pieces of "me" without my tag upon them. That's fine for "thee," but not for me. So I took steps to brand my ideas with my own special trademark, before I let them out of my grasp. Whether one was given directly to my boss or upper leveled over his head, I always loaded it down with an element of extra special risk. I made it just too dangerous for the guys up the ladder to latch on to it quickly. That is to say, I took advantage of the fear of failure up the line. Therefore, my name stayed hooked to the idea, in case a "fall guy" was needed later on. Cowards gain courage when there is someone to lay blame upon if things go wrong.

If you do not wish to run the risks of being a fall guy for your pet ideas, you are usually limited to following less spectacular methods of getting your new wrinkles considered. One, you can document quite thoroughly your recommendation in third-party language and attach a well-conceived letter of transmittal prepared on your boss's letterhead; both idea and letter can then be hand carried to the boss's office and given to his secretary with these words: "Miss Smith, here's something that the boss might like to read. Please tell him that I am available for discussion." By so doing, you can often provide your boss with the impetus to do something, if no more than to show the package to his boss on an informal, unsigned basis. Of course, this method will leave acknowledgment of your role or lack of it entirely up to your boss. Two, rather than upper leveling your own superior, it is quite possible to make like a sidewinder and plant your idea in another department. If you have good relations with men of your own level in another part of the company who might welcome such a new concept, you can very well get someone to informally discuss the thought with a higher boss in the second department who then might take it around the horn of even higher authority and back down to your own area. Many times, a new idea will gain intensity by such a process, but again, you will be at the mercy of others as to the revealing of your role in the idea's development.

Risky ideas are hard to come by with the bits-and-pieces method of putting new things in motion. A little piece of "me" will never get the company any part of my daring or my guts. A little piece of "thee" will never contain any part of your raw courage or your strength under pressure. It is not surprising that corporations get a reputation for cowardice, for most of the things they do are put together out of the flab, not out of the backbone of the men involved. Any man who decides to spend years in a big company has to make a conscious choice as to whether or not he will be a risk taker. Some can be happy never putting more than a little piece of themselves into any one project. Others need to do at least a few things up to their talent capacity and feel deprived when they have to water themselves down to fit some other man's image. Whichever you are, upper leveling will be part of your life. If you are happy as a bits-and-pieces type, keep the air full of trial balloons, but be prepared to have your thoughts lifted off those same balloons. If you are a guy who has to get some kicks out of giving birth to change as a one-man show, load up a few hydrogen-filled balloons involving much risk, but be prepared to have most of them blow up in your face.

Whether you specialize in little balloons with bits and pieces or large hydrogen-filled risky jobs, it is important to remember that it is the boss's fear of your making an end run that prevents his relaxed handling of all your ideas. The absence of a pure seniority system in the management structure of a big company allows brainy, young men to skirt their bosses, and it is just not human nature for a boss to let himself be outshown mentally by some guy underneath him. Most brains that feel threatened from below use heavy-handed methods in dealing with the ideas coming from the source of their discomfort, and many bright young people have become the victims of such bosses. If you have a superior who looks like the kind who can be threatened by the brain waves of underlings, the smartest thing to do is to clear the air by convincing your boss that there will be no run-around from below. Conversely, a boss who begins to feel insecure because of the emergence of bright, new brain power coming along behind him can best reduce his chances of being torpedoed by clearing the air himself. I have never known a boss to be hurt by freely passing on the ideas trying to fight their way up from below in his area, but many have hurt themselves beyond repair by trying to stifle bright minds under them only to have the brains being squashed find another approach to being heard. No matter how ordinary you are in the smarts department, Mr. Big, you can best protect yourself by being a free channel for ideas coming from your unit.

9

GOOD NEWSITIS

READ THE BUSINESS section of your local paper, and you'll see how cleverly companies handle the news about their results and conditions. In the giving out of dope to stockholders, customers, competitors, and the general public, good news is thought to be worth its weight in gold. Therefore, when there is anything bad to be dished out, it is very likely coupled with something at least hopeful, if not definitely good. Here's a pair of examples from the *New York Times*:

> The [XYZ] Corporation offered "disappointing" news but an optimistic outlook to about 100 stockholders at the annual meeting today. Chairman, [John S. Doe], reported that total revenues, net sales, net income, share earnings, production, and shipments of its products were all down from the comparable quarter last year.
> But, in his prepared remarks, he said, "I am personally encouraged by the fact that the last month of the quarter showed profits substantially better than they were in the first two months. Overall, however, I am optimistic and I expect a substantial improvement in our performance during the balance of the year.

If you read that rapidly, you probably didn't notice that the only thing that Chairman Doe had to make him feel optimistic was the horrible results of the first two months of the quarter, which he used as a base to make the less horrible third month look like an omen of improvement. Hardly a sign worth staking one's reputation on, but give the chairman credit—he at least put the bad news out over his own name.

> [ABC Gadget] Company, the third largest maker of [gadgets] in the United States, reported a 2.9 per cent dip in earnings for the period, to $230,000,000, or 84 cents a share, from $237,000,000, or 87 cents a share, in the same quarter last year. Revenues rose to 2.3-billion from 1.9-billion.

It was so hard to make that news look good that the man in charge of the ABC Gadget Company didn't even lend his name to the release. Bragging about increased revenues of $400,000,000 wasn't enough to make him want to tie his name to the news, for it doesn't take a genius to figure out that the stockholders were affected negatively by the results in the face of all that extra revenue. Oh, I know that the paper may have cut down on what it printed as compared to what it received from the company, but I would bet a thousand dollars to a plug nickel that the name of the top guy was not in that news release that probably came from some little man far down in the depths of the public relations department of the ABC Gadget Company.

So much for the way news is given out publicly. The above examples are mild forms of "good newsitis," but they are no more than an indication of what goes on inside a company to keep employees in the dark about reality and to keep the names of top men from being associated with bad news. Good newsitis is the management art of goosing employees with good news personally, while dulling their senses for the bad news by having some unknown guy put out the dope about what's gone wrong. I'm no prude when it comes to what employees should or should not know, and I have held on to my share of bad news, waiting for the tide to turn before saying anything. But I bucked like a bronco when my bosses tried to borrow my name to pass around bad news. Of course, I had to pass out my own bad news, for it would not have been cricket to make someone do for me what I refused to do for another. I don't bring this point up as a matter of personal virtue, but it does have a deep bearing on the kind of treatment that one gives to the management of the news.

Prophets like to sit outside the arena where the game of life is being played and make predictions about its outcome. When I am not responsible for results, I do not mind one bit acting like a prophet and guessing what's going to happen. It's particularly exciting to predict gloom and doom, for "I told you so" is much more dramatic when things go wrong. But like most prophets, I am usually in a foreign land by the time the story is told. While prophets can guess and run, leaders have to stay and face the music. As a leader, my job was to deal with the situation I faced, be it gloom, doom, or zoom. I would have been damning myself with faint praise if I put out any word at all about already present dirty linen or working messes, let alone saying how bad things were going to get. Therefore, nobody heard much out of me about the trouble at hand until the bad news had been turned into good news. News of trouble met and whipped is good news, so I have no bone to pick with other men who sit on bad news until they can flip the matter over to look better.

On the other hand, it may not be fair to employees to assume that they cannot bear up under tough sledding. To assume so is to brand them as fair-weather friends with no concern for the outfit and its problems. I have seen people kept in the dark for fear that panic would set in if the true facts were known. Two areas where top management is usually dead set against letting out the full facts to employees are cutbacks in the number of employees and reduction in sales costs. The feeling seems to be that news of a cutback in staff will make each person think he's on the list to be fired, and if the cost to move the products is reduced, people are supposed to instantly expect a drying up of revenue from sales. I am aware of the possible negative impact of these things on morale, but I have also seen the sad outgrowth of keeping bad news in these areas away from the employees. Put yourself in the shoes of a supervisor who is told on Friday that two clerks out of his twelve must be given two-week notices that afternoon. Is that all you want to know, or would you rather know something about the overall problem causing such a quick, drastic move? How about the manager in Kansas City who gets a call cutting his sales promotion budget in half for the next quarter, with no prior warning of any company cost bind? Would he grin and bear it, or would he begin to wonder why management is treating him like a kid who just found out he can't go to camp for lack of funds?

I have been left in darkness many times, and I have let the people under me wait for the rumors to bring them bad news on countless occasions. I have made mistakes on both sides of the coin when it comes to managing the news. I have loaded people down with disaster who never would have heard about it if I had kept my mouth shut. I have exposed many others to the sudden pain of being hit cold by hard facts when some warning should have been their God-given right. I have let men and women go ahead in expectation of good news long after I knew for sure that the opposite was true. Once, I even caused a bright young man to leave the company because he heard a particularly bad piece of news from me, which ultimately turned out not to be half as bad as it was thought to be. News! News! May it ever be good! And may all men who manage it have the wisdom to know when to let it out and when to keep it buried. May they also have the courage to strangle their urges to screw around with good newsitis when it means that some other men will be forced to take the brunt for bad news not of their own making.

I know one man who was made to carry so much bad news that he became a symbol of trouble. His boss was so anxious to keep his own love affair going with the employees that he used this particular person to tell it like it was— whenever the news was bad. But when it was good, Mr. Big himself was always right out there in front, oozing with confidence and thanking all for their roles in making the department so great. The man being used got to be known as a hatchet man when the most dangerous weapon he ever had in his hand was a ball point pen. Wherever he went, people put up signs, "Killjoy was here." A killjoy and a hatchet man rolled into one doesn't have much chance to move rapidly upward within a company in which being respected has a lot to do with advancement. That poor guy had about as much chance for promotion as an alley cat would have to run an asbestos rabbit through the fires of hell. Ask him how he got caught in such a spot, and he'll be the first to tell you that he fell into a trap, but he'll also talk at length about how he couldn't help himself. I agree with him that big shots do have a way of not saying or signing anything they don't want to say or sign, but some men under them do find ways to escape being used to pass out bad news. At least, they don't let their careers go down the drain.

For four years, I sat in territorial sales managers' meetings every quarter and watched a man by the name of Bert dodge the role. Whenever sales and costs were out of kilter, the department head would ask him to give the story on what had to be done to end the year in good shape. Bert was expected to come out with such things as cutting back on this and that to save some bucks, but all he ever said was that we had to get more business. If the boss wanted to cramp the style of territorial sales leaders, he had to do it himself. Old Bert wasn't about to help him, even though his job was cost control. He knew that putting teeth in a cost control program was the boss's duty, and he wouldn't pass out the bad news for him. The fact that Bert was allowed to keep his job is evidence that the boss knew it, too. So it is possible, sometimes, to resist being used. As for me, I would not be a boss's mouthpiece for bad news. I had enough trouble managing the news for which I was directly responsible.

In working out your own method for not allowing yourself to become a habitual harbinger of bad news, do not

overlook the fact that bosses are prone to somewhat reflex-
ively sign well-prepared letters or other documents. "Give me
completed work," is the battle cry of essentially all effective
executives. When I had knowledge of bad news that I thought
should be distributed by my boss rather than by myself, I
gave him completed work. In such a state, he had no choice
but to sign it or suppress it. In not one such case did a boss
ever throw a bad news item back to me for broadcasting over
my own name. It was in situations where my boss would have
knowledge of bad news before I did and would endeavor to
use me as the primary communicator that I would have
trouble avoiding the killjoy role. Every person in management will eventually face the challenge of not letting himself
be so used, and only your own diplomatic capacity to resist
can save you from the danger of becoming a hatchet man.
Avoid with a passion being used the first time, for the second,
the third, and the fourth become successively harder to skate
around.

Staff officers, as opposed to line officers, are most open
to the ravages of a big boss's good newsitis. They are charged
with smoking out bad news and calling it to the attention of
the guy in command. When they do their duty in such a job,
they are right there in the top guy's view and often become a
vehicle for passing on whatever was uncovered in the way of
bad information. While a staff man has no power and acts
only for his boss, he can still get branded as a bad guy if he
does fall into the trap of passing out the leader's dirty dope.
The staff man loses plenty, but the greatest loss can be to the
company. When such a man is used a few times to spread bad
news, he may very well cease to be good at his job. Disgusted
at having to give out the lousy side of the news, he may find
it harder and harder to come up with anything bad, and I can
assure you that no news is not necessarily good news; certain
things may be going to hell in a handbasket. While bad news
may be a hot potato to management, it is far safer to know it
and to manage it in some way than it is to go humming along

in ignorance, doing nothing about it. I wanted my staff to "sing," not hum, and to act as informers, even if it meant that I had to give up smiling to start bitching about the bad news they found.

Many companies have installed music boxes over which soothing tones are played at intervals to change the mental pace of the employees in the interest of getting a better work rate out of them. This sound system can double in brass and act as a speaker for the quick spreading of news. I give you my word that I have never heard any voice on ours except the chief executive's, and I have never heard any news but good news. If the building was on fire, the box would probably be working over the brain waves of the employees with "Indian Love Call," while news about the fire would start as a rumor in the men's room on the fourth floor and spread gradually through the building. No one would want the top guy to have to yell "fire," but nobody else would be allowed to use the squawk box. So the place would burn down while Nelson Eddy or Johnny Mathis or some other cat with a soft voice crooned. News! News! May it ever be good, but when it's bad, let us keep on humming.

Because the United States government is like a big corporation with everlasting life, you will allow me to say a few words about good newsitis on the national scene. One of the largest items in the news is the very treatment of the news. Many leaders in Washington, joined by millions of private citizens, are convinced that the news media of all kinds are so wrapped up in their own thing that objective reporting is no longer possible, if indeed it ever was. But there are just as many people in all walks of life who think that the present administration in the federal government is trying to control the news. These people applaud the media for giving the president a hard time. Now suppose the United States was really a big business and that Richard M. Nixon had the power vested in the chief executives of big companies. What kind of news do you think you'd be hearing? Spiro

Agnew wouldn't have to contend with his "effete snobs" for one moment.

Now I don't know about you, but I'm perfectly willing to admit that Dick and Spiro may have the spotless character needed to run this country as a business, but I feel better knowing that the cameras of NBC, CBS, and ABC are sticking their snouts into the places they want to go, rather than where Henry Kissinger and the rest of the White House aides might send them. In fact, I wouldn't want Fulton J. Sheen and Norman Vincent Peale telling the news media just where to be and what to shoot. Joseph Stalin and Adolf Hitler were pretty adept at managing the news. Forgive me, chief executives of American business, for such a tasteless reference, but in your domain, you have comparable power to that enjoyed by those men. I don't envy you as you manage the news in your company. Here's hoping your news is good news.

10

SOPPING

IT WAS ALWAYS easier for me to "sop" one of my children than to quiet him some other way. I found the all-day-sucker route less tough on me as a parent than trying to explain to a crying child why he should keep his mouth shut. Filling up his mouth with something sweet would take his mind off his problems and get him off my back. However, born with some of my finagling genes, my kids soon learned that they could graduate from the one-cent suckers to the gorgeous, multi-colored, three-inch jobs, usually found at carnivals and fairs. All they had to do was holler louder and make noise longer to come up with one of the super-duper kind. Buying bigger suckers was easier for me than cracking down on a child to keep him quiet or to make him mind. Frustrated, disappointed men in business soon learn that there are very expensive suckers on the market and that the more upset a candy-carrying manager becomes, the easier it is to latch on to some of the bigger suckers. Crying is out, but there are much more subtle ways to make a boss fidget and reach for the candy bag.

Any outfit in business that wants to be able to fill big job vacancies with good people has to have more talent on hand than it has big jobs to fill. There is no other way to make sure that a good man is in the wings when death, or something else, leaves an unexpected opening in the management ranks. For this reason, each man joining a big company starts out with the idea that there are far more big jobs up the line than there really are. The recruiting pitch is never toned down about opportunity; the men coming in are allowed to draw their own conclusions; few ever think the limit is less than the sky. You can be a colorblind, black, Jewish, fifty-five-year-old mail clerk in a carpet company in Alabama, and the guys who hire you will let you think that the way is open to the top spot. No recruiting process sets any limit on where the job can lead. Limitations might dampen the spirits of the guy being brought in to fill it. In fact, you can be passed over for promotion three times and be put on a permanent shelf, and nobody, but nobody, is about to tell you that your future is not bright. Sopping, then, is a way of life in big business.

The one-cent sucker of corporate sopping is lunch with some big boss farther up the line. Off in some private company dining room or in some rather swank eatery, the talk is about Babe Ruth, Willie Mays, and Hank Aaron, unless one of the two men loses his cool. Either the frustrated person starts setting the stage for giant suckers, or the big shot gets annoyed by the man's composure, be it real or feigned. The first to get away from baseball is usually the one to lose his grip. If the disappointed guy makes a move to show his distaste for the way he has been treated, the boss just lets him talk. An hour or so later, the guy finds himself out on the street still babbling. He goes back to his desk feeling no less irritated nor any more sure of picking up a sop. If the boss drops the baseball talk and begins to show wonder that the guy hasn't put in some kind of a bitch, he'll find himself coming around to giving something away, even though the man didn't ask for a thing. I learned on my first disappointment that one must not break the ice in such situations. I did so and found out that the boss took my bitching as a sign that I couldn't take it. This sign served to confirm his feeling even more strongly that he was right in not giving me that raise or that promotion. I wised up and thereafter let the boss squirm first. He could keep his one-cent sucker of a lunch; I would keep my cool and stir up a hornet's nest later for some real sugar.

At least I'd leave him with the problem of not knowing my true feelings. The only thing he knew about me was that I had a right to be upset, for had the shoe been on the other foot, he would have been mad as hell. So I would talk about when Hank Aaron could be expected to break Babe Ruth's home run record and let the boss think about what it would take to make himself happy if he were sitting in my seat. He'll have a tendency to be kinder to himself than to me, and the first sop will probably be bigger, if he figures out what he would want if he were me. If he is sitting there thinking that he would quit if he were in my shoes, my next raise will choke a horse, providing, of course, he wants to keep me around. In any event, I am not going to open my mouth to take on any one-cent sucker. It's going to take a pretty good sweetener to reduce the crappy taste in my mouth, but Mr. Big will have to guess for a while as to just how putrid my mouth feels. As I smile it up about good old Babe and how I hope his record holds, the big shot is sweating out my true feelings. Even if I am completely at peace, he doesn't know it.

If I succeed in getting him to return to his desk in an uncertain mood about what to expect out of me, he will find himself looking for a way to make me happy—to sop me up to what he thinks will keep me plowing ahead. He can find me another piece of money somewhere. He can find me a country club initiation fee. He can send me off to a fine executive development school someplace, even though he has no plans to use me in any newly developed state. I will enjoy the paid vacation that such provides and might make a contact worth something in the future. He can find some extra expense money and let me live it up in an unaccustomed manner on the road. He can work out a lateral move for me and give me a raise that could not have been given where I was. He can take something away from someone else and give it to me, expecting less static from him than from me. Here, of course, is where the real evils of sopping start; one man's earned reward gets turned into another man's sop.

Let's assume that a particular company has enough merit increase money to take care of five top performers out of ten men in a certain job level, if past policy for increases is carried out. I am one of the top five guys and top management doesn't want to lose me, even though it has just picked a younger buck to put in charge of the ten. Mr. Big Shot drags me off to his downtown luncheon club to feel my pulse. We spar around about the Mets, the Nets, and the Knicks and finally go back to the office at three in the afternoon with me smiling and him boiling at my lack of concern about having to report to the new young guy. He almost wets his pants when I drop this little bomb, "Mr. Jones at MNOP Company thinks the Mets will win the pennant." Mr. Jones is the big boss's counterpart at our friendly competitor. To his dying shame, the boss may very well go back to his office and decide that four raises are enough, load me up, and crap all over one of my friends. If he does, I'll be laughing as I do less work for my doubly increased pay. My friend will now have to work out his own sop. Hope he's as good at it as I am. Oh well, every man for himself.

Let's roll this back to where the basic problem starts: leading every man on the scene to think that he is ticketed for the stars. I saw a really fine performer sent out of the home office to be a territorial vice president, with two minds at opposite poles. One, the company had decided that he was going out to his final resting place. Two, he wanted with a passion to get back to the home office in a bigger job and felt qualified. For two years, he kept his New York State driver's license in force to avoid having to take a retest when he returned. When it came up for renewal the third time, he called the executive vice president on the phone and asked him if he thought it was a good idea to renew it again. Being afraid to dampen the guy's enthusiasm, the V.P. said, "Sure, why not," or at least that's what the man in the territory thought he said. A little later that year, the field man suggested to the company president that a change of some kind be made. Mr. President said, "When you get back to New York, you can make a project out of that idea and see if it has worth," or at least that's what the man in the territory thought he said.

See any sopping coming up? It was a black day at Black Rock when a younger thing was brought in from another territory to claim the big home office job that the first man thought was promised to him. The executive vice president flew out to the Midwest to see if he could get the one-cent sucker in the man's mouth, but he found his jaw set. While I wasn't there, I do know the talk finally got around to the weather, for it wasn't long before the guy got a lateral move to a warmer clime along with one of the largest salary increases ever given out in that job. If you think that some other man didn't get screwed, then you don't know anything about salary increase budgets in big business. Such a pile up of new money has to be scraped off the smaller mounds planned for others. In fact, the most deserving territorial vice president in the company didn't get a dime that year, and had his delightful one-cent meal later on—breakfast, no less. Sop! Sop! Sop! The executive vice president could have qualified as an honorary flagship admiral on some airline, just flying the suckers around the country.

And the funny thing was that none of it was necessary; the guys involved were not babies. Neither did they have my bent for making top management squirm. They were good, hard-working men who sought fair treatment, like most of the guys who enter corporate life. Just as strong kids take pride in jumping up from any kind of a fall, tough men prefer to fight off their prideful hurt without too much help from their bosses. After I learned to sharpen my sweet tooth at the expense of my superiors, I threw away my all-day suckers and learned to lift men over their rough spots with little more

than a smile of understanding or a few kind words. Oh I
know you can't eat words and smiles, but the guy on the
receiving end doesn't feel as if he has been sopped into a
state of obligation. After I found out how to maximize my
benefits from making bosses squirm, it lost some of its charm,
for my ass was obligated to a degree. If there was anything
I didn't like, it was obligation, and I was glad to find that
most men hated it as much as I did.

But regardless of how much we hate it, we aren't likely
to throw back any raises or turn down anything with sugar
dripping from it into our mouths. Give us candy, and we'll
take it. Stuff us with benefits because you don't think we can
handle our own frustrations, and we will soak them up and
hate your guts for robbing us of our manhood. Shower us
with honey to take the sting out of our wounds, and we'll
buzz around like drones, stuffing our guts and doing less
work than before. I have never known a pissed-off and
passed-over feast to go uneaten, but I have never seen such
a spread lead one to more loyalty or more devotion to duty.
In truth, most lead to contempt, particularly if the man being
fattened up knows that he is eating food that rightfully
belongs on somebody else's table.

Then, why do so many managers in so many companies
do so much sopping? I can only speak about my own urge to
sop, but from where I sit, it is due to the search that every
man conducts for power and glory over other human beings.
Just having a job does not seem to be enough. Title alone is
as useless as the tits on a tomcat; power comes from control-
ling others as an outgrowth of being in a job. If I had the power
to promote a man or to excite him in some other way, I had
control of him right away, but if I used my power to pass over
a man for promotion or to withhold from him to serve my
own end, I stood the chance of losing control over that man—
a clear loss of power. The very act of carrying out my duty
could reduce my power, if I made scads of people mad while
increasing the ties I had to a few—thus, the tormenting urge

to sop the multitude who may not like the way I pass out the spoils of my position. Maybe the sops will be enough to keep the majority within my base of power, though only a few chosen ones will ever really share my glory. One thing is for sure, I don't pass out any favors for what they will do for you. I pass them out for what they will do to the recipient and for me.

Few companies will possess such manpower strength that sopping will disappear, but in the faces of real men, I have seen the horror at being bought. And in the faces of weak managers, I have seen the horror that comes from being in charge but not in control. While sopping will not make permanent peace, managers will continue to use it in an effort to maintain their power and glory. The cost in dollars to companies can be fairly accurately measured, but the drain on the self-respect of both the men being sopped and the managers doing it can not. Sadness creeps into the hearts of each, and the company loses much of the vital energy of both parties. If I go on television's "Let's Make A Deal" as a guest, I expect a handout; if I go to work for you, I expect to earn what I get according to the rules of the business. If I am the master of ceremonies on some give-away show, I expect to pass out the goodies and kiss you goodbye; if I hire you to do a job, I'm hoping to be man enough to keep your respect and to maintain my control over you out of my fairness and ability. Sopping cuts the rug from underneath us both as men and robs us of personal pride, even if it lines our pockets.

11

SALARY SUCTION

DID YOU SEE in the paper where Sugar Tit Corporation's top guy got paid $812,494 in 1971, up from $766,775 in 1970? The article went on to say, "His nine top executives earned from $121,373 up to $342,060." Not a bad team to be on, but it's not all-upmanship that we want to examine here. Suffice it to say that those nine guys draw their pay from the company, but their asses and their souls belong to the man on top. There may be a few souls that won't sell for those prices, but there isn't a rear end in the free world that can't be had for over a hundred grand. Hooray for the team, but it's the snowballing effect of "salary suction" to which this chapter speaks.

Top management doesn't have to sop itself; it isn't mad at anything or anybody. However, it does have to wrestle with the very real problem of how much to pay itself. Being in charge of fixing their own salary rates exposes them to the threat of greed on the one hand and the chance of being too modest on the other about their worth to the company. Believe it or not, there are known cases where men have held themselves down in pay with an almost unheard of constraint, but top leadership usually goes overboard in its own favor. In itself, this deed is not too bad for the company, for the number of men at the top is too small to drain the kitty dry. In the case above, knocking a million dollars out of the total pay of those ten guys wouldn't put one cent per share on the dividend checks of the owners. It is the suction upward of each job level's pay rate on the one below it that compounds the compensation problem and runs up the cost of management, often out of all proportion to its worth.

To clearly pinpoint how this suction works, let's stick with these ten men for a moment. While Mr. Big obviously thinks that he's worth as much to the outfit as any three or four of the others, he does have to pay man number two a whopping $342,060 to keep himself from looking like the most self-oriented man in civilized society. Even then, there is a vacuum, crying to be filled, of over $450,000 between the two men. If you don't think so, just wait until you have paid the price to become number two. You will be expecting leverage in your back pocket to salve whatever wounds you bear from having been a most active player in all those corporate games over the years in which the top boss has been your coach. You'll know a lot of history worth a lot of money not to be told. You'll have money coming for having performed certain duties so confidential that you couldn't be paid at the time you did the "work," if that is a good word for such service. And you will be expecting the boss to suck your salary up now for old times' sake. He, of course, knows the history as well as you do, and he was the one who profited from your behind-the-scenes, as yet unrewarded, activities. He can hardly ignore your attempts to play on his downward loyalty to fill the gap between your pay and his. Not only that, you will also have one of mankind's strongest urges going for you, his desire to come back to the pack after he has gotten so far ahead of it. It's that great social awakening we all get after we have it made ourselves.

No man will physically turn around and come back to the pack; he will slow down and let the pack gain on him. In this way, he can stay whole himself and still thrill to the progress going on behind him. Yes, Mr. Number Two in the Sugar Tit Corporation, great things are in store for you. You are sitting just outside the opening of one of the biggest salary suction vacuums on record. Keep your nose clean and your mouth shut; look for a new house in the Caribbean; and find some more tax offsets. You're going to have money running out your ears. In fact, your pay is going to get so high that number three man is going to become a problem. After all, you have been taking your frustrations out on him, for it would not have made much sense to bite back at Mr. Big when he gnawed on you. Face it, you owe number three more than peanuts. When he sees your move into the vacuum over you, he's a cinch to want a piece of the action. Think he'll get it? If you are not some kind of a freak, able to bleed bosses without giving out a drop of blood yourself, he will. One little, two little, three little Indians; four little, five little, six little Indians; seven little, eight little, nine little Indians are all going to have their assets increased. From "ass et" to "asset" is no more than closing a gap.

The two largest raises in my career came from salary suction, not from my own sparkling performance. And would you believe that I wasn't even fishing for them at the time? All I had to do was sit there on the bank of the stream and grab the silver-sided beauties when they jumped out toward me. The vacuum between my salary and the guys just ahead of me got strong enough to suck the fish right out of the water. I didn't throw them back; I preferred taking them home and putting them on the table. Since I wasn't of the ten top indians, salary suction was starting to dip pretty far down by the time it got to me. For sure, it was clearly out of the chief's tepee into the operating departments, where guys like me were supposed to have the guts to stop the snowballing and nullify the effects of the suction. Along with my raise came some encouragement to hold the line below. It went something like this: "One of the reasons you get paid so well is because you have the job of seeing that those below you don't get more than they are worth, and remember that we can't give you any money that you give to the guys down there."

No one had to tell me that it is not possible to pay two men with the same dollars, but I sure did need to have someone show me why I was expected to have the courage to stop the salary suction underneath me, when the so-called strong men top-side couldn't do it themselves. I, too, had my obligations to others and my desires to be liked. I had my social consciousness and impulse to let people gain on me, now that my own pockets were so full and my own cup was running over. The gap between me and "my guys" (yea, team) became too great. There was no way that I could tell them to go jump in the lake when they brought their buckets to the money well. And I could be sure that the buckets would be lined up all the way to the bottom of management. What a switch on the old-fashioned bucket brigade. I would have had to start a fire to put out the buckets. I never had the will nor the strength to do so. While I didn't share my own two fishes with the multitude, I most certainly showed them where to pitch their own nets to take advantage of the currents flowing into the vacuums lying around.

My company was nowhere near the giant size of the Sugar Tit Corporation, but it did have about three hundred men in management in the home office, along with an increasing group of very capable women. There were no salaries of gigantic proportions and nowhere close to ten indians making over a hundred thousand per year. However, two or three twenty-five thousand dollar increases were dished out over the last decade, with their full impact on salary suction. If each triggered an average increase of $700 all the way to the bottom, they had a rather large effect on total management pay. I wouldn't swear that the effect was that big, but I can say with no fear of being refuted that a lot more money was paid to a lot more people, including me, for no more output in time or effort. Oh sure, it was a period of great inflation, but what in the name of heaven was causing the inflation? Was it the cost of labor or materials, or the extra money paid to management as an outgrowth of salary suction? The welfare state of the nation is getting no less for its money than the welfare state of a company when its top boys give themselves bigger salaries and trigger raises all the way down the ranks.

Corporate ballplayers are like many professional athletes. They often have their worst seasons right after getting their largest raises. But even if one has his best, most gratifying time right after a big raise, it is not the money that did it. Yet top management is forever telling men at salary increase time that it is expecting increased productivity, even though it knows itself that it can't work any harder for its own bigger pay. As the gravy boat comes sailing by, it is followed by a tug, tooting its whistle for harder work and more output. To dedicated management men, this tooting should be an insult; at least it was to me. From the day you enter the ranks of corporate management, you should be involved daily up to your physical capacity and reaching for more mentally challenging duties. If you are not doing these things, you shouldn't get any increase in pay ever. So let's get this straight—management salaries are not pay for time and effort. Therefore, salary increases cannot be for increased productivity. Both are for the role you play in getting work out of the workers, and neither comes from working yourself. For these reasons, salary suction has such a profound effect on inflation; all that new money gets paid out without a single worker processing an extra sheet of paper or sewing on one more button. No wonder labor is always bitching about management when it hikes up its own pay. Labor knows it isn't going to work any harder, no matter how loud the call to do so from management. And if the situation is any different with white collar workers, I never saw it. If the workers are good, a managerial off-season doesn't hurt the company much.

Put another way, Salary Suction only leads to higher management cost for the same output. Therefore, it should not be billed as a stepping stone to higher productivity. I put in no more time and effort after my salary was sucked up than I did before, nor did I succeed in getting those under me to work harder because I was making more. Three hundred guys were managing away while top bosses made up their minds as to how much of the total revenue they could gracefully take for themselves. Once decided, they made themselves respectable by taking care of the chosen few next to the top and hoped that the vacuums opened up below didn't get fed too full. I was one of those chosen few, so I'm not complaining in any shape, form, or fashion. I would have gladly voted for any man's salary to go down except mine, but for me to make what I made, both those above and those below had to get about what they got. Would you believe that real management ability had little to do with it in either group, and surely not with me. If I've got the job, and the suction starts, I will come into my two or three huge fishes often enough to keep me around. Conversely, if the suction is there, and I am being regularly left out, it should be a sign that top management has decided that it doesn't care to cut me in on the increasing revenue. In truth, it may be a sign that they would like me to hit the road.

Speaking of hitting the road, I note a rage among top management in big businesses today to sweeten up the early retirement features in their companies. The changes in the world are so rapid that no one man can keep up with them over much more than twenty years as far as they apply to any one company. The men who latch on to the top power spots in big business know their own inability to keep pace, but they are not about to turn loose the reins. They do not want to maintain a second layer of obsolete guys right up under themselves to place their own ignorance in double jeopardy, so most guys like me will be encouraged to move on. During the time between my expressed intention to bow out and the actual point of departure, my good old company changed its retirement privileges at age fifty-five to such a degree that my pension rights went up forty percent. While I would have gone peacefully at the old rate, another fish jumped out of the water into my basket. Bless their hearts for my good fortune, but the change was made to set up a series of departures. It's a kind of salary suction on a retirement basis for the good of the company. I can see more good there than some of the changes I saw set off as full-fledged, all the way down the line handouts, after top management opened up the cock on its own sugar tit a little bit too wide for its own comfort.

12

FIRST GUESSING

EVERY HIT RECORD has a flip side, which may or may not be a fitting partner for the front runner. Try these combinations for crass mismatching of tunes. The national anthem of Israel on the one side and "Let My People Go" on the other. "We Shall Overcome," as sung on freedom marches, coupled up with "Old Black Joe." "Let Me Call You Sweetheart " paired with "You Ain't Nothing But a Hound Dog." "Dixie Land" on the one side and "Marching Through Georgia" on the flip. "I Love Life" and "The Prison Song" make an interesting combination, not to mention "Born Free" hooked up with "Turn Me Loose." From where you sit, you can decide which is the hit and which is the flip in these tune tie-ups, but if you are a big shot in big business cutting a hit record, you may very well scratch out a sour companion tune on the back. You can start out with your company's fight song, determined to overcome all obstacles, bouncing along like a sweetheart, whistling Dixie, loving life, and free to do anything you want, only to end up feeling like a hound dog, with a noose around your neck, saying to somebody up the line, "I'm coming, I'm coming, but my head is bending low."

For me, the thrill of leadership is risk taking, and I considered it the only way to cut much of a hit record on one's own. However, I was not so keen about the flip side of risk taking: blame taking. Lucky me, I had sprouted my eyeteeth in the army, where protecting one's rear becomes a way of life, so I brought an instinct into business for ways to block off blame. But I also knew about the valuable trophies that risk taking can throw off when things go right. I had seen a corporal take over an entire infantry company, including its officers, and be promoted on the battlefield to officially take command. I was also aware than an insignificant lieutenant colonel by the name of Dwight David Eisenhower, from a standing start before 1940, had gone all the way to president of the United States by taking risks. Suffice it to say that I was ready to "Sing, sing, sing a new song," while setting up that old refrain called "Don't Blame Me" on the flip side. The trick of the risk-taking trade is in making sure that your song of victory doesn't turn out to be a dirge on the way to your own burial ground.

Second guessing is the simplest form of "don't blame me." It is so easy to say to a guy down the line, "If you want to try that, go ahead, but I don't think it will work." If the man has the guts to proceed in the face of my weaseling second guess, I enjoy the best of two worlds. I can take credit for having the wisdom to give the go-ahead sign, if he succeeds. And I surely can place the blame on him, if the idea bombs. But it's easy to see that second guessing isn't going to lead to much risk taking, either on my part or by the men under me. When I got the old, "Go ahead, Joe, but I don't think it will work," treatment from my bosses, I muttered something about "gutless bastards" and went underground, waiting for a more fitting time to get the idea started. That time comes when one has a boss who really is hungry to cut a new hit record and is willing to play a game called "first guessing" to do so.

First guessing is not the simple airing of doubt as a hedge against the chance that something will backfire; it is the secret, precise action planning done in advance of launching a risky project, action that will be unveiled and pursued if failure strikes. If things go well, no one will see these plans. The top guy will bask in reflected glory, and everybody connected with the deal will come out smelling like a rose. But if the music does turn sour, out will come the first guessing plan and off will come the head of some predetermined John the Baptist who let himself be put in the fall guy role. Such plans make it possible for companies to undertake more risky ventures; they supply the courage Mr. Big needs to try anything more than routine.

The foundation stone of first guessing is the fall guy. Unlike certain Orientals who in the past have been willing to take a sword and dump their own intestines on the floor in the face of failure, we Occidentals prefer to chop up somebody else. I sure as hell wasn't interested in hari-kari, but I didn't look forward to having my throat cut either. Some of my bosses had so few guts that not even hari-kari would have killed them, but those same guys were in a position to turn my head over to some belly dancer gladly, if my preaching led the company down the primrose path of failure. One doesn't have to fully qualify as a coward to shrink before such odds. Given a choice between life and death, even the strong seek life. So where do the fall guys come from?

Some are anointed; some are appointed; some volunteer. I have seen examples of each that I will get back to discussing later. Let's take a look at the potential for personal gain that being a fall guy can place at your doorstep. If I provide a boss with a way out for himself, thereby giving him the courage to proceed with a big risk, he will feel some obligation to me if the project strikes a mother lode. Some of the ore that comes out of it will find its way into my pocket, though my role goes unrevealed. In fact, a surviving fall guy must learn to keep his mouth shut about his role, for no boss will appreciate having some other man sounding off about how he gave management the guts to go ahead. Fall guys should fall out of sight and wait patiently for their rewards, unless their bosses decide to share their glory with them. First guessing is designed to let the big guy act like a risk taker without fear of failure; the fall guy who comes in after the fact to try to grab off some glory the boss doesn't want to share is committing suicide. I believe in keeping quiet to pick up whatever spoils come my way in money, promotion, or power.

There is also an intangible reward, if you can get your own pet project tried out in the process of being a fall guy. If I had not been willing to serve as the escape valve for my boss, I would have absolutely nothing to show for my twenty-two years of corporate life in the way of creative, innovative, new methods of doing things. I say this reward is intangible, for I feel very strongly that my pay check would have been essentially the same if I had never reached for a new idea. No matter how the dollars may have gone, the fact remains that I was forced into the role of fall guy by my desire to see some of my own unique thoughts get a chance to prove themselves. I quickly admit that I lacked the courage to risk being the fall guy for all the ideas I had, but there were two big thrills in two decades, as I have mentioned before. By playing on my boss's willingness to engage in first guessing, I was able to get those two projects out of the dog house into which they had been ho! ho! ho! downed.

Once a senior vice president of a major company was anointed a fall guy for his president. The president got a bug up his butt to change the basic merchandising pattern of the company, for which the senior vice president was responsible. One day, an outside merchandising expert walked into the senior vice president's office and used the president's name as a referral. After the senior vice president got up off the floor, the expert proceeded to show him what the president liked about some new concepts. Any idea what you would have done under the circumstances? The senior vice president decided to like them too, and took on the role of fall guy before he could get the outside expert out of his office. The fact is that he hated the man's concepts as well as his guts, but didn't have guts enough of his own to defend himself. The project failed, and the senior vice president had to hit the road. To my way of thinking, he was lucky to get away from that kind of leadership, but I don't know how he feels about it. Anointed, disappointed, and disjointed, he made par for the fall guy course.

The difference between being anointed and being appointed is in knowing what's going on. The poor guy who gets anointed doesn't know what hit him, but the man who is appointed to be an escape hatch for his boss will be in on the decision and could probably turn it down, if he wanted to. (All one has to do to bow out is to insist that the assignment be put in writing. No Big Boss will do that and the deal goes by default.) Few do, for the rewards can be great. Also, refusal would not further one's career. So when a young man was asked by his boss to head up a research team to check out the development of a new gadget that would be named for the boss, he jumped at the chance. The boss never mentioned the project to anyone else, for he preferred not to let people know that he wanted a monument to himself in the product line. The young guy was no dope; he knew that anything as full of dynamite as developing and naming a new product after the big boss was no small potatoes. He really worked on the gadget, and when Mr. Big asked him to come forward with the idea of making it, naming it, and selling it, he could see the cash register ringing. He was appointed by the boss to be the fall guy, and he agreed willingly to keep the old man's name out of the deal. It was easy to get the rest of the top management team excited about surprising the boss, and after all, Mr. Young Guy was ready and able to serve as John the Baptist, if one were needed. They didn't know about his previous appointment by the old man himself. Don't fret, things went extremely well. The young man is miles ahead of where he would have been if he hadn't been appointed the fall guy.

The essence of volunteering to be a fall guy is having absolute faith in the idea you are willing to back with your whole career. After having my two pet projects ho! ho! ho! downed, I upper leveled them all over the top management structure, and got nowhere. Years were involved in this process, but I was finally able to set the stage with a boss for first guessing in each case. The two men who were my bosses at the respective times each needed a project with more than a small potential for making a sizeable wave around the place. I volunteered to run the show on each project and to sign every paper ever put outside of the department on the subject. In the meantime, both of them kept their bosses verbally informed of what was going on. Even when one has a fall guy, he has to be careful not to get caught with his trousers at half mast. You already know that things went well for me on these two deals and that they gave me my proudest moments during twenty-two years of everlasting corporate life. Praise God and pass the recognition; first guessing is a great game, when you win.

Do you want to make some hit records as you sit around for your twenty or more years, feeding on the corporate body? If you do, you better become aware of first guessing as a vehicle for moving your ideas along, but don't lose sight of the flip side of risk taking, blame taking, even in singing minor tunes. "Clippity clop, clippity clop" is a catchy part of Frankie Laine's song about a mule train. I used to use his tune and put in "flippity flop, flippity flop" about some of the horses' asses who used to blow with the wind around my company. But I can't resent them very much, for life is no bed of roses for leadership in any field. Sing your song, cut your record, but don't ignore the flip side. Management has to first guess before it shoots from taw, and fall guys will always be in demand. I can only point out the need. It's up to you to decide on the tunes to which you are willing to dance. "Fool train!!! Flippity flop, flippity flop."

13

PYRAMIDING

WHILE A SINGLE thread of life can lower a man down into a pool of people to sink or swim, he has to build some platforms to keep himself afloat. We all scratch hard to do just that, and we throw up platforms of family, religion, community, and business, among others. As politicians know better than anybody else, these platforms are made out of people. People hold a man up, and they can pull him down. I don't mean to beat on former President Johnson, but he found this fact out in spades. In any pool of life, when the people who put a man where he is decide to bring him down, down he comes. His platform collapses and his deeds become memories. This is the story of most men's lives who climb to platforms of corporate glory: the people put them there, and the people can bring them down.

In business, the height of one's platform is greatly determined by what management up the line thinks about him, but the strength of his position has more to do with what the people down below think. Top management is known for putting men on platforms of great height, only to find out that the guys and gals below don't share their opinion about the worth of the men uplifted. In a company I know about, through the power of the chairman, a man was put in a high place. The people festered but didn't say or do anything for a rather long time. Business was good. In fact, the chairman had reason to be proud of his man, but the people kept saying to themselves and to each other that things would be better if they had new leadership. Mr. Big kept on adding to his guy's platform, not knowing that the people were silently siphoning off their support from below. At a large companywide meeting, some self-appointed spokesmen started bending the chairman's ear about how ineffective the man was. Later on, the big boss swung around the field to see if the feelings were widespread. He found his man's platform swaying like a forest fire lookout tower with two legs cut completely through. If you don't think the people brought him down, you have not seen a top dog move in such a case. The man was now a termite, eating into the big boss's own platform. He went fairly quietly.

Most men see that staying afloat in any pool requires a solid platform, and management men in business try hard for real strength underneath themselves. However, few are ever satisfied with the height of theirs, and the urge to do some "pyramiding" can become great. If I do not think that my platform lifts me to my proper place in the sun, I will try to build my own little do-it-yourself pyramid to push myself farther up into the atmosphere of personal glory. And, believe it or not, the higher my solid platform becomes, the more I seem to need the upward hoist skyward. Not even the chief executive of a gigantic corporation really feels that his role in the world is as great as his ability could have made it, given just a wee bit more power. Once on top of the platform known as the total company, he cannot escape feeling the need to expand his personal impact. Pyramiding will often look like a quick way to more power and glory, particularly for a man who is slightly over the hump agewise. Rather than add on a solid tier of new company growth, the top man will throw up some three-sided, styrofoam structure to con people into thinking great things are happening.

After breaking through the Siegfried Line in World War II and dashing to the Rhine River, the infantry division to which I belonged found itself on the west bank opposite the town of Duisburg. The bridge had been blown, so we were the width of the river from that city of 500,000 people. Down came the word that no one was to cross the river until further orders; the general wanted to take personal charge of our next move and rightly so. Our battle plan had run out at the river's edge, and crossing over into the heartland of Germany was no small step. But there was no shooting coming from the other side of the great Rhine River, about which every young American of that time had read so much. Curiosity got hold of two cats with lieutenant's bars on their shoulders, and they went merrily rowing across the Rhine in a bateau. Word got back to the general before their feet hit the soil on the other side, and he issued orders to have them arrested and delivered to his headquarters for trial the minute they got back. In the meantime, the two guys were met on the bank by the bürgermeister of Duisburg, taken to city hall, and welcomed.

Word of this went back to the general, and he couldn't resist the urge to pyramid. Rather than slap our two oarsmen in the military clink, he met them in front of his command post and pinned Silver Stars on them for gallantry in action, while the cameras clicked. Not only that, he put news in the *Stars and Stripes*, the G.I. paper, that the division had captured Duisburg. A platform built on the solid task of bursting through the Siegfried Line, crossing the Roer River, and dashing to the Rhine was just not high enough for the man. He had to pump up a pyramidal-shaped crock of horse manure on top of his truly fine record in an effort to get more glory. The rest of the armed forces may have been impressed, but the people who brought his butt to the banks of the Rhine were not, even though we were glad to see the two guys escape trial.

In war, declared or undeclared, there are all sorts of pyramids, from body counts to new invasions, but the military really can't hold a candle to big business when it comes to a leader's urge to grab off power and glory faster than his solid platform can generate it. There can be pyramids of new ventures, purchases of other companies, industry recognition, political ambitions, social causes, outside directorships, and just plain old profiteering. None of these things, from starting something new to making profits, is bad in itself; it's their self-indulgent use to a high degree by a business big shot in the name of his occupation that turns them into pyramiding. To blow up his own tepeelike air bubble on top of his platform known as the company, Mr. Big will commit resources and assign people to a project far out of balance to its worth to the whole. As long as he can keep the impression going that the deal has merit for the outfit, not just for him, he can stay up on the pyramid. However, when people learn that personal glory is the main thrust behind such a move, the pyramid may come tumbling down. Worse yet for Mr. Big Shot, he may take a fall. In this case, one of two things can happen; he will fall forward and slide on his knees to the bottom of the pyramid, or tip backward and get the point up his rear end. Either smarts.

One of my pyramids was raising money for my local church. Every fall for six weeks, I gave more energy to the church's financial drive by far than I did to business. My secretary typed reams of church stuff and kept the company's duplicating people busy on things of no worth to the outfit at all. "Who hasn't done this?" you say, or something like it. Probably over half the people at the vice-presidential level, at least. I cite this little, rather insignificant individual matter to bring out the accumulated effect that a hundred or more men can have on a company by spending hours or days on things designed to play them up personally in some church, charity, or social club. I have no argument with the worth of their causes or the needs being served; I am only saying that business picks up a very large tab in time and money for things out of its own realm.

The Eiffel Tower of all pyramids is buying another company in a line of business completely foreign to one's own field. One of the great rages in American business today is conning one's self into thinking that the top level ball team in management is so strong that it can take on the direction of a new company with no sweat. The truth is that Mr. Big has loaded up the superstructure of the outfit with more team members than he really needs to run the company, and he is looking for some extra things for them to do. He runs out and buys another outfit, only to realize that the idle hands he has don't know sand from Shinola about running the new purchase. Instead of being able to cut the management staff of the added company to bring around the profits on which the wisdom of the deal was based, the pyramiding chief finds that his team is so inept that a third group is needed to keep the lines of communications open between the two companies. Each top team is so threatened by the other that cooperation is impossible, let alone peace. When a tire and rubber company buys a stock brokerage house, crossbreeding management becomes some kind of a headache. Maybe adding an aspirin maker to the mixture is a good way to get the show moving. Chances are that the bleeding hearts and heavy-handed people making up the frustrated managements of these companies may see their marriage as undesirable and do nothing to hold the pyramid up.

Have you noticed the tepee villages of outside directorships springing up all over the business community? Top indians are lending their basic platforms to each other and each is getting his extra kicks out of throwing up a pyramid on somebody else's reservation. The close-cropped Hurons of the financial world are slipping quietly onto the land of the long-haired Mohicans in the garment industry to pitch tents in exchange for hunting rights on their own land. Scalping is not the mission of either party, but the tribes suffer the loss of their chiefs' time and counsel. It's not uncommon for a chief to have as many as six tepees pushing up out of somebody else's dirt. In terms of dirt, it is a good thing that directors of big companies are so remote from the hunting grounds of day-to-day activities that they are not held individually responsible for the lost hides and missed meat of the tribe. If it were not so, these traveling pyramids of self-indulgent big chiefs would disappear from the scene. The risk of sharing their great personal magnetism with other friendly chiefs would be too great for the small value of the wampum expected in return. These guys don't like risk at home; they surely won't take it on the road for beads and trinkets of personal glory.

Sammy Davis is a runt of a man, but among entertainers, he stands exceedingly tall. Yet, one will hardly ever see this song-and-dance giant without his platform shoes. Even he has this thing about standing taller. Compared to Davis, the run-of-the-mill executive in big business is small in talent for his role. No two-inch platform shoes for him; he needs a Cheops pyramid to get him off his low level platform of unsung corporate glory. Even if he's in charge of the whole thing, he seeks something outside of the company's normal pursuits to boost his ego. I had my fling at roaming off the reservation in search of personal game to put in my own coonskin bag, while letting my company pick up the cost of my extra movement. So I really had no complaint when bigger indians than I started to rustle around far afield, but I balked like a wild mare when some chief tried to take me along on one of his foraging trips to hoist his own ego. If I was going to make like an Apache in Cherokee country, I wanted to hang my trophies from my own tepee.

Not only does today's top management have to deal with its own urge to push up peaks of power for itself, but it must also cope with a social demand for quickly erected A-frame-like efforts on top of its basic platforms. The public, from whom all revenue flows, is getting more and more raucous about what it thinks a big corporation should be doing on social issues. If top management does not listen to these pleas in such things as ecology, public safety, and fair pricing, it may find its basic platform eaten away by decreased income. However, if big shots with the urge to pyramid get carried away with some of these chances to shine in the public eye, it may set their companies back in a big way. For instance, there could be a social cry for big business to play a large role in licking the drug problem. If some top executive turned his company into a Synanon-type haven for addicts, as a stepping stone to his own glorification, he might end up digging a hole in his platform instead of building a pyramid. Not only might he suffer, but the company might suffer badly as well. While this example may seem far-fetched to you, there are other things less dramatic that business must leave to government. For instance, each individual business on the shores of Lake Erie should stop dumping polluted waste into that lake, but none of them should undertake the task of filtering the water already there. Such a move would break any company, but the United States could do the job.

Oh yes, I know the poet was right when he said that every man's reach should exceed his grasp, but clutching for personal glory at the expense of one's company is not what he had in mind. I have attended more than one testimonial dinner where some business big shot went home with a fifty-dollar plaque for toting acorns to a blind hog for twenty years, which must have cost his company over a hundred grand. I know one man in a company other than my own who spent his life in charge of pyramids. His top management used so many pyramids in their search for personal glory that the guy became a vice president just designing such structures for his big bosses. They showed up to break ground, lay the first stone, and dedicate the structure, but he took care of everything else, including the very extensive publicity on each one. Unlike Don Quixote, who lost his mind chasing windmills, this fellow found his "impossible dream" building three-cornered outside houses for his bosses whose own dreams should have been satisfied by the solid platforms of their big jobs. Pharaoh he's not, but he built his share of pyramids, some of which turned out to be tombs.

14

POPULARITY EXPLOSION

ROGUES AND DESPOTS are seldom popular in a free society where word about their mischievous, hard hearts can get around. As I sought a base of corporate power, it was clear to me early that I would have to steal about like a rogue on occasion and clamp down like a despot at times. Yet some degree of popularity was also needed, if I was to get a big job. How to be part rogue, part despot, and still be fairly popular became one of the great juggling acts of all time. Bosses greatly admire your larceny and toughness, but they also expect you to keep the respect of the troops below. You cannot be an outright thief or an unmitigated son-of-a-bitch and still be liked, so bosses think that the urge to be popular will tend to keep you honest enough and soft enough. It does, too, but there are times when your popularity has to be given special treatment to make it match up with the plans to promote certain people. Top management likes to have a big job appointment accepted by employees with some degree of excitement at the moment it is made, so at that moment, it helps to have a popular guy to put in. The process of rigging a man's reputation to peak his popularity at the right point in time is a "popularity explosion."

I have been the object of such an explosion, and it's fun. I was wrapped up in a glossy package and put on display by a boss who thought that he needed me to take over his slot in case he could get his foot into a bigger puddle. Each corporate big shot is led to believe that his own advancement is going to be delayed until he can get his successor lined up. Therefore, much time is spent grooming a man to take over, and part of the process is the plan to explode his popularity at just the right time. In my case, my boss got surprised. Out of a clear blue sky, it began to look as if his own boss was about to get knocked up a notch. Bless his heart, my boss got caught with his pants down, so to speak, and didn't have his successor properly combed and curried, much less popular. In his eyes, I was the best guy on the scene to get ready in a hurry. He didn't call me in to reveal his plan, but the signs were there, and I wasn't about to turn down the chance to vault ahead. First, small firecrackers started popping all over the place. I was asked to show up in meetings that normally would have been shut to me. I was put in charge of the department's five-year plan, which is a sure sign of confidence. I was sent to top management on matters that had previously been reserved for my boss alone.

Then, the rumored promotion of my boss's boss happened, and my popularity explosion had to begin in earnest. My boss, the poor guy, should have known when he was not elevated at once that I was not going to fly with management as his take-over man. However, hope was beating hard in his breast, and he fired up the rockets to explode my popularity anyway. He moved me into his office, which he vacated to go sit where his boss used to sit, thinking that seeing me there would give people some extra respect for my future in the scheme of things. I found it hard to see how the private john was going to add one whit to my qualifications for leadership or how it could bring me any extra respect from the people who were using the common facilities on that floor. As you have already guessed, he had to back me out of this office later, but I'm not through telling you about the final efforts he made to get me popular. There were more assignments designed to show me off, but the final horns, bells, and whistles deal was his effort to show top management that the field managers could stomach my promotion.

To do this feat, he made me the keynote speaker at the upcoming meeting of those field sales managers. Again I say, "Bless his heart." It took guts for him to do that, and I decided to really pour it on. I'd be holding something back from you if I didn't conceitedly tell you how I felt when I came down off that dais. I was walking on air from the applause, but I knew the popularity explosion had just peaked too high. Sitting out in that audience were too many men with more rank than I who never had been allowed on that speakers' rostrum, not to mention the ones who had been, only to do a lousy job. Tiptop management isn't about to breed too many speechmakers to compete with itself. Charming that audience didn't reduce the fears that top management had about me in that promotion, it only made them more resolved not to use me. I have to respect their judgment now in hindsight, for the man who can move a group by oratory will get support for his wrong programs as well as his right ones. But at the time, I was convinced that I made that speech too good for my own good. In my juggling act, I had thrown the ball of popularity too high. Regardless of how you look at it, my boss had picked the wrong horse to back, and his heavy betting on me had only served to lengthen the odds. My one experience with being the object of a popularity explosion was over, and my poor boss had to wait years before he could prime another boy.

Explosions like mine go on as a way of life in most companies, with varying degrees of bang and often only fizzle. But the granddaddy of all such pows is the one staged by a newly elected chief executive officer who has some fear about his own popularity. Applause he knows he can get, but if he feels in his heart that there are very good reasons for many people not to like him, he will campaign for employee goodwill. When he does, the explosion will rival the noisiest Fourth

of July in your memory. There will be a long period of fanfare, followed by a massive blast, much like an inauguration
or a coronation. The fanfare has two main elements. First,
there is the negative part, by which other men of high rank
are made to look less able than the guy taking over. These
men are coaxed into activities with which they are not familiar, only to end up looking like dunces. Nobody likes a
dunce, so their popularity wanes. Second, the new top guy
becomes Mr. Nice Guy and starts building fences with all
parts of the company which may have reasons to hate him. A
close look at what popularity really is will show you why a
man in such a spot will drag others down as well as build himself up.

Politicians know that popularity is the excess of goodwill over bad, which is why they take such close looks at public opinion polls. They also know that their star can rise in
relation to another's, without actually moving up on its own.
One man's popularity can be enhanced by the lowering of
public esteem for another. Is there any surprise, then, that
political campaigns see mud slung at the opposition as well
as lures in the form of sweetness and light staked out for the
public? Is it any different in business? You can bet your life
that it isn't, and the mudslinging and luring do not stop after
the top job is filled, any more than the political arena goes
silent between elections. Mr. Big will never stop trying to
outshine the other men around and will keep up both the
negative and positive sides of the fanfare. The boss knows
that popularity among the Boston Strangler, Jack the Ripper,
and Adolf Hitler, if people had to choose, would be decided
by which was thought to be least evil.

Here's a neat little way to blow one's own horn while
cramping the style of every other officer at the same time.
Issue an edict that home office people traveling in the field
will not be allowed to pick up lunch or dinner checks for salesmen or sales managers, and see that the controller enforces
the rule; then go into the field yourself and pick them up all

over the place. If Jack Benny had made his living dealing with field sales people, he would not have lived to reach thirty-nine, but you can be Diamond Jim Brady by comparison if you carry out this little trick. Decide in your own mind that the company is going to be forced to improve on its physical living quarters, but for the record, hold tight to the old standards. In this way, you can require every executive below yourself to be a hard-nosed, hold-the-line guy on increasing space and comfort, but you can spread around joy through making exceptions at your level only. Many a top man has maintained his hero image through the management-by-exception route. Take a tour around the building and ask this question over and over, "Joe, is anything bothering you?" If you were Joe, would you miss the chance to spout off to the big boss? Would you bitch about anything that you thought Mr. Big himself was doing wrong? No, you would complain about things that he could go back to his office and use to jack up some other big shot. You would help him with his own fanfare, without really knowing what kind of a game he was playing.

We could go on, but so much for the fanfare. What about the massive blast so necessary to cap off every top-level popularity explosion? There'll be a parade, for sure. Conquering heroes like nothing better than to stand in triumph as their subjects march by, but in business, the boss usually does the moving and the people stand still in meetings or banquets. A kind of reverse twist, but a parade, no less. Leadership without public exposure is like marriage without physical love: how can employees know how great one is, if they haven't felt his presence? But once having felt his presence, the crowd wants to see the cut of their leader's cloth. Is he a petty thief? Is he a benevolent despot? If he's a thief at all, will he scrounge for them, or will he take from them? If he's a dictator, will he jam things down their throats or will he grease the rod of reality to ease their pain? Needless to say, he wants to start out popular. Before the noise of the parade is over, he will set off some kind of moon shot, powered by a give-away program. There are lots of good fuels for such rockets, like a salary increase across the board, or a new profit-sharing plan designed to give everyone a piece of the profits if last year's results are merely sustained. There's no shortage of fuel; he's had it tanked for months. Start the countdown.

T minus ten, nine, eight, seven, six, five, four, three, two, one, BLAST OFF!!! Mr. Big is off and soaring into earth orbit for a temporary hold, before deciding what to do next. If there is enough money lying around to pay for a second-stage rocket, he will probably fire on off toward the moon, if the people have firmed up their loyalty in stage one. However, he could be in earth orbit without the wherewithal to go any higher, making it necessary to cut off the explosion. If he is, he'll find that his need to abort the mission due to lack of cash has set him back to where he began in popularity, if not farther. Unlucky is the man who lights up a full-scale popularity explosion and runs out of funds before he can really put the crowd in his camp. Such a man may end up wishing that he had laid low until his popularity could have been born out of solid on-the-job action rather than the contrived ransom he paid. But it takes a strong man not to give in to the temptation to rig his reputation and to peak his popularity as he takes over a company. Why?

Any man with enough experience to take over a big company knows that he will make many errors as he moves ahead. While he truly believes that he is the best man available for the job, he will not expect to do everything right. He will have seen other men—good men—in the job who have missed the mark of excellence on many occasions. He will have seen tough cookies turn to jelly rolls in the face of hard facts, and go limp when backbone was needed. He will remember giving his full support to men he thought worthy, only to find them less than worth it. He will have seen men take over the company riding high in popularity but destined to stump their toe on some minor matter, with great loss of employee respect. He will have seen at least one man of vast ability go down the drain of personal weakness with his hand in the wrong drawer or on somebody else's woman. In short, Mr. Big knows the odds against his performance improving his reputation or his popularity. Can he really be blamed for wanting to start out being admired? No, but he must be sure that he doesn't trump up popularity in some manner so temporary that the odds will go up against his growing as a man in the eyes of the company masses. At best, one of the prices of leadership at the top is living to see one's popularity wane. Why would any man want to start out with an undeserved halo, just waiting for it to be knocked off? He may as well have a chip on his shoulder.

15

TONGUE GASHING

"TOM, TOM, THE piper's son, combed his hair with a wagging tongue," is a line from an old childhood ditty. Like so many things from way back then, that song has dropped out of sight and hearing. But there is one thing in this world that will never change: man will forever be getting his head creased with a wagging tongue. Yes, and his wrist slapped, and his tail chapped, and his mind blown, and his heart broken, and his hair curled, and his eyes watered. Talking and being talked about on one's own terms can bring kicks that every man loves, but having to talk by another man's rules or to listen to another man put you down is sheer torture. As in all walks of life, words are a dime a dozen in business. People are prone to talk and anxious to listen. If gossip and rumors were the only results of such talk, it wouldn't cause problems, but the tongue can be used as a weapon in a vicious game called "tongue gashing." I found my tongue a weapon in most scraps with other people. Winning a battle of wits is great, but I had to use my tongue to really wound. Not only that, no one would have known that I had stabbed a guy, if I didn't crow about it.

Back to the bullfightlike precision of premeditated tongue gashing later, but first, let's look at the cutting effect of careless, unthinking talk. I have had so many lessons in why one should not open his mouth and let his random thoughts run out, that I should have learned long before I entered business to think before speaking. I wish you better luck than I have had on being able to do so. Irving Cohen was just about my closest friend at the hottest stage of my combat experience in Germany. We captured a certain town and found it blown to high heaven by very accurate army air force bombing. Everything was leveled, except an almost untouched munitions plant in the center of the place. Sitting in a cellar, eating out of mess kits with the commanding officer and his staff, someone was curious as to how that gun factory was missed. I was Tom, Tom, the piper's son, combing my hair with a wagging tongue, saying, "Oh, it's probably owned by some Jew back in the States." Irving Cohen jumped as if he'd been stabbed. As a matter of fact, he had been. Then it became the role of the tongue to change quickly from a dagger to a medicine brush to soothe the hurt in Irv's wound. Poor old tongue, it has to play so many roles. How's this for balm? "Irving, I am so fond of you that I don't even look on you as a Jew." Ouch!!! The dagger now had a fish-hook on the end and was getting harder and harder to pull out of my "friend." By this time, Irv was damn glad that he wasn't my enemy.

In the world of big business, there is so much tongue gashing that many people seek outside therapy to offset the effect of inside talk. Guys sneak off to head shrinkers in bigger numbers than anybody cares to think about, and there are literally droves of executives popping up in T groups and other sensitivity sessions, not to mention the hordes going on retreats of all kinds. Talk seems to be the only avenue to overcome personal problems, most of which begin with talk in the first place. Men go off to talk to strangers, professional and otherwise, in search of relief from their own verbal venom as well as from the cutting remarks of their company mates. It's kind of a jawbone therapy for jawbone wounds, many of which are self-inflicted.

I never took a trip in quest of help to lick my wounds, but I have sat in lots of corners mumbling to myself as a way to recover from welt-making words. Once I made a strong argument in support of an idea, being very careful not to step on any toes, much less tongue gash anybody. The group was surprised, for I wasn't known for my tact, preferring to let the chips fall where they might. Maybe my new-found concern for the feelings of others was too much of a surprise for the biggest boss present, but here's what he did when I got through. He walked up and shook hands, leaning forward in the process to say in a very low voice, "Listening to you put me in a mood to take a crap." The rest of the guys didn't know whether he had praised me or not. If his tongue hadn't been so tightly tied to the back of his lower jaw, it would have been sticking out of the front of my body. I made like Little Jack Horner for some time after that, but I was not using my thumb to pull out plums. It was too busy trying to stop the flow of blood oozing out from between the second and third ribs on my left side.

Later on, in another matter, I had my chance to gash back at that boss. He put me in charge of a sizeable project and called a meeting to see that all the other high-ranking men involved understood clearly that I was his man for this deal. I could see that he was trying to be helpful, but the hole in my chest was still draining from the old wound. After setting me up royally for the success of the project, he asked me in open meeting what he could do to help. I hadn't been sharpening my tongue for nothing, and out came the words, "The best thing you can do is to keep your hands out of this deal until I can get it done." Every man in the room except the boss wanted to applaud, for he could never let one of us really run anything. However, none so much as smiled, for each knew that my remark was uncalled for and didn't wish to share in the boss's reaction to my inane utterance. He, of course, kept quiet, but now I had a hole in my back to go with the one in front, put there by my own tongue. Back I went to the corner, this time sucking my thumb like a child, while I bled from the back. In passing, let the record show that just because words are founded in truth doesn't make them easy to take. That boss knew he was the meddling type, but he didn't want to hear it from me.

When one wants to use his tongue with the precision of a matador, he plans carefully. He selects an audience favorable to his views, picks an arena on home grounds, lines up his attendants, hires some picadors to upset the victim, and writes his script in advance to hone the cutting edge of his tongue. If he doesn't do all of these things, the bull he's trying to stab just may put a horn in him. Ask America's most decorated soldier in the Korean War, Colonel Herbert, how it feels to go after a bull in his own pasture, surrounded by thousands of fellow-traveling, four-footed creatures with sharp horns, without one single friend, and with no help at all. When in Viet Nam he tried to accuse the army of covering up atrocities which he had reported, he found his one-man effort brushed under the rug. After long pursuit within the military framework with no results, he polished up his tongue and went to the press, gashing out at specific individuals in the army as well as the outfit itself. He learned quickly that when a man uses his tongue for a dagger, he may very well stab himself. Whether he was right or wrong in his accusations is not the point here, but no one should have been surprised at his early retirement from the service.

While I was in charge of a territory for my company, a man was hired to change some of our basic sales procedures. He was not a company man, and I didn't like him personally, let alone respect his ideas. Rightly or wrongly, I made up my mind that he wasn't going to enter my domain, but how to keep him out posed a rather big problem. Sooner or later, I was going to be forced to gash out at somebody, and up to then, I didn't even know who hired him. As the deadline for using my tongue to head off this guy stood staring me in the face, I learned that the chairman himself had dug the man up.

But by this time, I had lined up my supporters, selected an arena on my own grounds, armed the picadors, and written my script. It was too late to call off my planned outburst which went something like this: "I do not want that guy in my territory; measure our results without his help, and I'll stake my future on outperforming the rest of the company." Thank God that the field managers in my territory carried out their promise to do just that. They saved me from stabbing myself, and helped me gash that particular bull with precision.

At work, try to go one minute without talking. If you are in a position of general management, the odds are great that you cannot do it, unless you force your secretary to cut off the phone and guard your door. The function of people like you is to meet the daily events in a company and see that things are dealt with in a timely way. You cannot put everything in writing to help you weigh your words; you must use the spoken word to carry on your day-to-day duties. Out of those duties comes your contact with people, and your ability to talk almost constantly with respect for both your own position and that of the other man is the key to being a topflight manager. As I have told you, I had mountains of problems in this regard, and I tried to play take-it-back many times. Sure, I could take it back as far as I was personally concerned. Apologizing could get that done, but the people who hear you apologize are never the same ones who heard you pop off in the first place. Taking any word completely back is a physical impossibility.

When managers are talking about inventory, sales, costs, revenues, new construction, or almost any other business matter, they have reports to support what they are mouthing off on. This is also true in regard to the number of people on hand, but little is put in writing concerning what people are like or what one man thinks of another. If you can get a look at your personnel file, you will find no more than a series of forms filled out by various bosses which say nothing about the real you. Yet you are the subject under discussion on many a sober occasion as your bosses try to figure you out in an effort to make the best use of you. As careful as they usually are to document everything of importance they say or do, bosses just do not make their thoughts about people a matter of record. I know from years of being part of the verbal evaluation system that a man's imprint as a man on the minds and hearts of his fellow managers is a word-of-mouth thing. What Joe thinks about Bill may take up an hour in the boss's office, but don't waste time looking for any record of it; it's in just such meetings that Bill can get stabbed.

It's easy to see why most of the lying around a company has to do with what one man said, or is reported to have said, about another. When faced with that nasty question, "Did you say that about me?" it's so much easier to lie than to face the music. After one such experience, I learned not to try to run down who said what about whom. If there has been any tongue gashing, adding on a layer of lies will not bring peace nor salve any wounds. This lesson also taught me that if I was going to spew out words, I had better be prepared to live with not only what I said but with what people thought I said. I also began to see why so many managers mealy-mouth through life, never saying anything of much value. However, I could seldom tell whether such a guy was sincerely afraid of tongue gashing somebody or didn't have the guts to take the consequences.

Take the consequences; that's really the crux of this whole matter. The guy who said, "Sticks and stones may break my bones, but words will never hurt me," must not have spent much time working in a big company. Maybe other people's words won't hurt, but if you aren't cut from your crotch to your appetite by some of your own, Gunga Din, you're a better man than I am. Here's hoping you are immune to the acid barbs of your fellow man, but immunity will not prevent you from tongue gashing others. Samson reportedly killed many Philistines with the jawbone of an ass. Watch out that you don't use the same weapon on some of your business associates.

16

EX RATING

EX MEANS "WITHOUT the right to have." "Ex rating" is the permanent dubbing of an individual or group by some privileged person or class as, once and forever, "without the right to have." Since the beginning of history, most big social issues have boiled around some version of ex rating, often to the point of war. Our own Civil War is the classic example to Americans, but there is scarcely a nation that hasn't written some kind of chapter in its record book in this regard. Look at today's struggles; so many are being fought over "the right to have." Women's lib, civil rights, gay liberation, gypsy cabs, prison reforms, and abortion laws are just some of the current crop of issues where people are clamoring for the right to have. Maybe some of the things for which people clamor aren't even good for them, but in the eyes of those being told they cannot have, the telling is the most degrading thing in life. Such people would rather run the risk of graduating to heroin than to be denied marijuana, chance syphilis than to observe sexual caution, head up a window-breaking expedition than to obey a law that has nothing to do with the institution whose windows are being smashed, or sit down in front of a bulldozer rather than let it bury their right to have a little piece of grassy land forever.

This book is not about morals. Choose whichever side you wish on these or other issues; picket, demonstrate, civilly disobey, or stick with the party line, as you see fit. But this book is about power in big business and its effect on those who have it and on those who don't. To firmly relate ex rating to power, let's look at one more historical social issue. In its early years, Christianity was run underground, and Christians were denied the right to have many things they wanted, like free worship and churches of their own. Later on, when the power swung, people who called themselves Christians denied rights in the name of Christ to many others. Yes, ex rating is a function of power, and those who have it will never stop dubbing those who don't as, once and forever, "without the right to have."

Of all the powers known to man, the power of a management man in big business over those who report to him comes closest to sheer autocracy. Labor unions were born to get people out of this chain of power and to insert a contract between the two parties which would clearly define the working man's "right to have." In the management ranks, no union is likely, for power begets power, and no professional manager will agitate for a system that would clip his own wings if he be lucky enough to stumble onto a higher power base of his own. It is exciting to know as you start out in management that you will be the king of the castle in your domination of the people below, that your only restraint will come from above. This you can take, for you fully expect to rise to greater heights yourself. Also, the right to have, at even the bottom rung on the corporate ladder of power, is pretty large. Managers of the lowest order are too privileged to picket, plant bombs, or organize against those of a higher rank. However, many are ex rated and denied the right to have by "bigoted" bosses who apply their personal likes and dislikes in the wielding of their power.

For the pettiest of private reasons, a big shot will slam the door of advancement in the face of a capable man and will hold on to the notion that no more progress is possible for years. Not only that, he will put the word out to other executives between himself and the ex rated man that they too must turn their backs on the poor guy. Having tried on several occasions to get an ex rating lifted, I can vouch for the almost impossibility of freeing a man from such a freeze. No boss between him and the problem guy will risk his neck to crack the ice; he might get ex rated by association. If you try to promote a man who I think is unworthy, you take the chance that I will doubt your judgment and will be reluctant to approve your future recommendations. So, if you know that I don't want to see a particular person make any more progress, you will deal him out yourself.

Of course, no one is likely to tell a man that he has been ex rated; it might make him lose interest and slack off in his job. His bosses most certainly do not want this to happen, and he'll never learn from them that he has a problem with anybody. They will push him hard to become more effective, and he will do so in hopes of advancement, not knowing that a top performance has no chance to pull his chestnuts out of the fire. He'll get fine ratings on his job record but will live to see men with no more talent go streaming by on the organization charts. Extremely deserving men can grow old in such a fashion, never having reached a job that demanded anywhere near their full ability. And would you believe that some of them stay on with the company out of loyalty to the very piss ant who ex rated them in the first place? When the Bible says, "Love your enemies," the man speaking probably expected one to know who they are. If not, there had better be room in heaven for all these guys who love their corporate enemies, without knowing who the hell they are.

When a man who later became president of his company was V.P. for sales, he hired a good man from the Oh So Peachy Company, Inc. The guy brought a lot of know-how to his job, but he was never able to forget where he learned it. Every time the boss heard him say, "We used to do it this way in the Oh So Peachy Company," he had a conniption fit underneath the surface, but he never did let the man know how he hated to hear those references to a competitor. It would have been so easy to stop, but the boss never tipped off his dislike. To say that the poor guy got ex rated is putting it mildly. He hadn't moved a notch by the time Mr. Big got to be president, even though his bosses just above thought highly of him. To this day, he loves the man who took him out of the Oh So Peachy outfit.

I used to ride the train with a man who couldn't understand why he wasn't making faster progress in his company. One day he said, "Maintaining enthusiasm in the face of indeterminable obstacles is escalating my pessimism." In other words, he was teed off by no progress. I said, "Why don't you go in and blast your boss to see what's the matter, but you had better be ready to look for another job." He had his head-knocking session, and the boss finally told him that the man upstairs couldn't stand all his big words. He had been ex rated for reaching so hard to appear brainy. Now he had to decide whether to change his words and hope for the better or to make a move. When he asked me, I said, "Hit the road; once dead, always dead." Since he didn't work for me, I could be as open as a book, but if he had been in my company, I would have probably encouraged him to stick it out in hopes of a change. He quit, brought his words down to earth, and his salary went up by sixty percent in two years. Underneath all those big words, there was a pretty good guy.

When neither the man nor his boss knows that a guy is ex rated, many trips can be made to the well of promotion, only to find it dry. I pushed Champion over and over for a bigger job to no avail, in spite of his good record and ample fitness for the larger spot. After try number three, I got tired of being stalled off for no real reason. Under some heavy pressure from me, my boss told me that he couldn't dare promote that guy because of the president's feelings about him. That wasn't enough for me; I had to know how the president felt. After more jawing, my boss finally said that he had heard the president say, "Goddamn that Champion," over three years ago. He couldn't remember why, but he wasn't about to take a chance on what Mr. Big might think about Champion today. Even though the promotion could be approved far below the president, my boss knew that the company newspaper would carry the story and tip off the head man, who might be upset. Man, if that isn't once and forever "without the right to have," I can't visualize what is. Champion needed a "champion"; I took on the assignment and got the job done on try number five.

Of all the reasons for ex rating, refusal to move from one city to another is the most out-in-the-open cause. Most individual moves are part of a chain, one link in a series of location swaps. A boss will set up three or four job changes involving a move in each slot. One man's refusal to pull up stakes will foul up the entire plan. Before any one man can be asked to move, top management has to approve the whole shebang. When doing so, the big boss likes to say to the man in charge of getting the men to move, "I bet you a cigar that Jack won't go." In other words, "You better see that all these cats get up and go." The man in charge is given the idea that his own future is on the line. In a case like this one, there is no greater fly in the corporate ointment than a guy who says, "Hell no, I won't go." Ex rating is mild treatment for such an offense against the everlasting corporate body.

I was moved seven times by my company, but it would have been eight if I hadn't refused to go. After seven moves, my income was high enough to give me a don't-give-a-damn attitude, and I just decided to take my chances. If top management wanted to ex rate me at that salary level, they could go right ahead and do it. Besides, the move made so little sense for me personally that I could visualize the president having predicted in his cute way that I wouldn't go. If he had done so, I could stay put and still not have my future shut off to advancement. After I said no to the move, my boss paid me a very solemn visit, saying, "This will affect your future, you know." I considered how my future was affected every time I took a leak, as I sent him on his way. He wasn't around the company much longer, and I had guessed right. The top man had said, "I bet you can't get Murrah to go." To this day, I think that he was glad that I didn't go, for I got two more promotions after refusing to move, a rare thing in big business.

Please do not reach the conclusion that I think any man should have anything he wants in business or in other areas of life. Most certainly, everybody working for a company cannot be its chief executive. True, you can't make a silk purse out of a sow's ear, but if I'm a sow's ear, I sure don't want to be left out of the head cheese just because the butcher has a thing about not liking a brown hog. I am what I am, hanging from my temporary thread of life. If I touch down in a business pool with you, I would like you to respect me for my full potential and not to brush me aside just because you don't like the way I part my hair or the cut of my jacket. In other words, do not ex rate me for anything other than sound business reasons. Both you and I, boss, are sucking on the same life-giving, everlasting corporate body. You can well be entitled to a tit closer to the milk supply than I, but it doesn't give you the right to stand on my back to reach it. Suck away, big boy, but be prepared for me to get away from that hind tit sooner or later, even if I have to leave your company.

17

FUNNELING

WHEN I WAS young, I picked as many bones with the army authorities as today's youth do with what they call the "Establishment." If you don't think so, how does this grab you?

> I detest the tendency on the part of the army to discourage free thinking on the part of its younger officers. I am convinced that the longer a man stays in the service, the less intelligence, common sense, and mental capacity he possesses. After years of being bound by TRADITION and the limited elasticity of the usually narrow mind of one's immediate commanding officer, a young officer actually deteriorates mentally. I feel that I can leave the army now for twenty years, and that at the end of that time, I will be capable of returning to active duty in any national emergency better equipped to guide the destinies of American men than I would be if I remain in the service for the same length of time. In other words, I would lose so much flexibility of thought and so much actual mental capacity through the hidebound military ties of service that the small amount of military knowledge which I could and would obtain would be insufficient to keep my brain from shrinking.

In June 1946, that made Mark Rudd and Abbie Hoffman look like Sunday school teachers. Since I wrote the above in my letter of resignation to the Pentagon, there has been almost a constant need for infantry battalion commanders, but I'm not surprised that no one called me to help out, nor am I disappointed.

Having to pass my ideas through the mind of a man less aware of the need for new thinking than I am, has been a very bothersome part of both military and corporate life for me. I call this "funneling." By whatever name, it is the forcing of my thought processes through the more restrictive head of another man. I have no shrunken heads hanging from my belt as trophies for overwhelming anybody with intelligence, so this point has nothing to do with restrictive mentality. However, it has everything to do with restrictive viewpoint—tradition, if you will. In business, there is really no word to convey the same meaning that the word tradition supplies to the military. The military needs tradition to give it something to hang on to between wars. Business has no such need, for it is supposed to be stretched out to the limit of its capacity at all times, reaching for gems of thought to bring about change. I digress, but God forbid that the military would have to stay so constantly involved in combat that tradition would go out of style, replaced by the constant urgency of the moment, as in business. Oh, I know, you'll hear guys in your company saying that things haven't changed in forty years, but the fact remains that most big outfits make noble efforts to bring about effective change. They conduct studies, keep up operation research, and do many things daily to get a wide range of thinking upon any subject before the house. The bad part is the funneling that takes place in trying to harness the broad-scope ideas to come up with practical applications.

As the years piled up behind me in business, it became more difficult by the day to see things go by the wayside, things into which I had poured buckets of my sweat, if not my tears. One gets comfortable with the old ways of doing things and is prone to take his ease of operation for a sign that all is going well. If I happened to be in on the birth of today's trite practice when it was yesterday's bright new process, I am doubly averse to giving it up. If all I did was make like a midwife and give the new baby a bath ten years ago, I may have so strong an attachment to it that I will still want to keep it alive. Can you see how I can become an island of individual tradition in a surging sea of change and can turn into a full-fledged stick-in-the-mud in the eyes of people who have the vision to picture progress here and now? Before I stepped down from my company, I am sure that scads of people hated to have their thoughts funneled through my limited viewpoint as much as I despised having my pearls of wisdom pushed through the three-eyed coconut heads watching over me back in 1946.

If I decide to funnel something, I can squeeze the juice of creative new thinking out of it with the effectiveness of an old-fashioned clothes wringer. You're a bright new boy in my unit, and you come to me with your first brain child, born out of your fresh approach to one of our oldest procedures, one that I really love. Just in case you do have something, I agree to set up a three-man study group to check out your idea. I put you on it, of course, to make sure that you have a full chance to sell your thoughts. (Pardon me while I laugh.) Then I tell you to pick one other man, and I do the same. You look around for the shiniest embryo Einstein you can find, and I dig up the old codger who started the present program over twenty years ago and knows a thousand reasons why nothing else can possibly be as good. For seniority reasons, the old guy is in charge. The group meets once; Einstein throws in the towel; you come to me hollering "calf rope," which means I tied your hands. If you bitch too loud, I'll brand you as one who can't get along with people and who has trouble working as part of a group.

Back up a notch; let's assume the old-timer's mind is more open than I thought it was and that you and Einstein succeed in getting him to join you in an endorsement of a new procedure. The group writes up its thoughts and sends a report to me. You have high hopes, but you don't hear anything for weeks. During that time, I have met with the old guy and shaken his confidence by being very negative myself. Eventually, all three of you get a memo from me outlining my deep concern that what you have brought forward will not do the things you say it will. I suggest that you drop a part as being unworkable and take another look at the idea as modified. What I suggest dropping is merely the guts of the whole idea. Hell, I'm not funneling your thoughts at this point, I've got them blocked off completely. But you don't give up, for you still see a ray of light in the old man. After much soul searching, he rolls up his sleeves along with you, and back to me comes even a stronger recommendation that the change be made. Now I've got to use the facilities or get out of the bathroom, so I write you three again, saying, "Thanks for the time and effort put into the project by the group, which is now dissolved. Its report and recommendations will get further consideration." You don't know at this point whether or not I'll do any more than funnel it through my own head. If the old man's hanging in there has given me less reluctance to change, maybe I'll open up my mind a little bit and funnel it off to my boss with some lukewarm expression of interest. Being farther away from the point of use than I am, his head may have even a smaller opening than mine and be a tighter funnel yet. Write your own end to the story.

The final funnel for any idea is the top man in whatever unit has the power to say yea or nay on its adoption. To come about, anything new has to dribble out of whatever opening can be drilled into the viewpoint of the man who has the final say. If the people below cannot drill a hole of some size, the top man will be a plug in the flow of progress, not a funnel. My trouble in the army was typical of youth; I was not willing to sharpen my drilling bit to make a hole in my commanding officer's viewpoint. It never occurred to me that he didn't get where he was by being a sieve through which any old crap could ooze. I gave him no credit at all for shouldering the burden of slapping me down when I was off base, without cramping my style when I had something good to bring forward. The last man I talked with as I left the Pentagon to go home from the army was Lightning Joe Collins, a three-star general of great World War II fame. He said about like this: "If you think any other outfit is going to let you do as you please, you're crazy. But if you do find one that will, it'll be full of goddamn fools that you won't respect any more than you do the guys you worked for in the army." Thanks, Joe, you triggered my insight into the need to drill holes in my bosses' viewpoints to bring about change. Otherwise, I could not have made it in business. That insight gave me survival, but to this very minute, the thought of being funneled burns my butt.

Whenever my base of power gave me the final judgment on somebody else's thinking, I tried to remember that my viewpoint had to be breached, if correct change was to take place—that someone had to use a drill on me to open up a funnel through which progress could flow, no matter how slowly. As ideas were dumped into the hopper leading to me as a funnel, my "voice of experience" could be a pompous wind or a refreshing breeze, depending on what kind of an opening there was in my mind. Listen to some pompous winds: "Jesus, Jack, we looked at that five years ago. Have you lost your mind?" "I don't care what your tests show, as long as I'm in charge here, we are not going to stop that service." "Just forget it; the president started that in 1960, when he had my job. He would die if we took it out now." "The computer has taken over everything else around here, I'll be damned if it's going to gobble this up too." "That guy isn't dry behind the ears yet. Tell him to turn off his motor until he gets his feet wet." When I was young, I was always mixed up on where to be wet or dry. I used to laugh when the voice of experience said, "Don't pee down your leg," but seemed to want my feet wet.

But oh the joy in refreshing breezes: "Jack, we looked at that five years ago, but it cost too much. Now we have the computer; I would really like to have it gone over closely again." "When the president started that, there was a real need for it, but I'm sure he would be the first to want to see it go, if it's not doing anything for us now." "When we put that in, it was my pride and joy, but I have been hoping that you guys would challenge it in light of what the field has been saying recently." "How could a guy that young come up with such a promising new idea? Pull out all the stops and let's test it quickly. He may have struck gold." The voice of experience, as a refreshing breeze, can dry off a young man behind the ears in record time, and using one of his new ideas will get his feet wet fast. Who knows, it could bring showers of blessings on the company, too.

Being blessed with everlasting life, a big company can put up with funneling. Time is of no essence to the outfit itself, for change will take place at a rapid enough rate to accommodate the company. However, the rate of change is seldom, if ever, just right for any particular man. Irony of ironies, the young with the most time think the change rate is too slow; the old with the least time hate for the most part to see it speeded up. Twenty years gives a man a full dose of each and can turn a fine creative mind into a very restrictive passage. A funnel is a reverse trumpet. A trumpet makes music because wind is pushed into its little end by an expert, and his artful input gets tuned by the instrument to waft happily over the crowd. Funneling takes the wide-range knowledge of a group, drops it into the big end, and waits for the sheer weight of time to ooze some kind of voice out of the neck. The man opening the valve can make it a refreshing breeze or a pompous wind.

18

DEFROCKING

"IF I HAD enough arms and legs and time, I'd do it all myself,"
is a quote from the chief executive of one of the nation's top
companies. The feelings which caused him to make that
remark house the seeds of "defrocking." By virtue of his exalt-
ed rank, each manager in big business thinks that he can do
the jobs just below his slot better than the guys in them are
doing; so this particular big shot's urge to do it himself is not
surprising. "Anything you can do, I can do better. I can do anything better than you," is sung by Annie Oakley, who was a
mean hand with a gun. From her, it made great entertainment, but there is no more degrading experience in everlasting corporate life than to be "shot down" by a boss who not
only thinks he can do your job better than you, but also starts
doing it for you. Maybe he will not do it all, but at least he
begins to run off with the most exciting pieces.

I was breast fed on the Golden Rule, which eggs one on
to finger his fellow man in the way that he would like to be
fingered himself, but this training from childhood did not
keep me from blasting my boss every time he stuck his finger
into my soup while I rammed my arm up to the elbow into the
duties of my crew as the spirit moved me. "Thou shalt not kill,"
found its way into the basic rules of human decency before
the Golden Rule, but it gets its share of abuse in big business,
too. Unless one is moved not to kill, he will find it impossible

to keep his hands off the duties of those managers reporting to him. Any man swimming around in a big business pool of people is a candidate for drowning by a variety of methods, but being defrocked of his duties by his boss will send him naked to the bottom quicker than anything else. Men have stayed afloat for years with millstones of hate around their necks or anvils of envy strapped to their backs, but when their duties are lifted by their bosses, they sink. Solid performance in one's job is the only effective life jacket in anybody's corporate pond, and one has to sink, if his boss strips him of it. Throw me all the crud you wish, Mr. Big, but don't defrock me; that's murder.

As much as I hated to be thought of as a vicious manager, I was guilty of defrocking for two very simple reasons. One, I had previously held most of the jobs of any real importance below me. Coming through the ranks had made me very familiar with what the managers below faced—not the workers, the managers. Few of us ever steal any work. Two, I was promoted so often that I never got tired of the job I was leaving. Under these conditions, one has to be dedicated to another long-standing rule of human conduct. "live and let live." Man, that's hard. It really frosted me to be floundering around in a new position, groping for the keys to effective progress while watching some guy or guys below wrestling with alligators that I could have shot from the hip with ease. Annie Oakley nearly lost her lover by outshooting him and never would have bagged him if she hadn't finally let him master her performance. I had to learn that neither I nor my helpers were ever going to shoot well or straight with each other unless I stopped meddling. Living up to my job and not down to those of my associates was a must. Looking over a man's shoulder in a spirit of helpful interest is one thing, but physically poking one's finger into another's routine is deadening to his only human right not swallowed up by the everlasting corporate body: the right to perform his duties up to his ability as he sees fit. If he's not able, fire him, but how can he be judged if he is not allowed to show his stuff.

What does one do when his boss starts taking his job away from him? Does he scream hands off to the boss, or does he turn loose whatever the guy is trying to grab? It takes a lot of courage to even hint that your boss is off base as he snatches something out of your hands. But hinting will not be enough to stop the guy, anyway; a tug of war is the only way to show your disgust properly. However, there is no guarantee that pulling back on your part will see you keep your duties, if I as your boss, set out to take them away from you. By the law of corporate practice, I own you, lock, stock, and barrel. Think you can make me behave? I don't recommend your trying as a way of goosing your career, unless you know that my power base has already had the flesh picked off its bones by a bigger buzzard than I am. Since that never happened to me, the guys that I defrocked just had to grin and bear it.

In the face of my taking over the guts of their jobs, they had no choice but to reach down and strip the job-rights from their lieutenants. Otherwise, they could not fill up their own day. It's sad to reflect on this now, but I have seen this pansy-chain go all the way to the bottom of my unit. I say pansy-chain, for how I wish that somebody had had the guts to fight back, instead of letting me rob them of their manhood. In the absence of the courage to fight a defrocking boss, a man has no way to stay afloat except to strip his underlings. If he dares let me take his job and lets them keep theirs, he's out of business—putting in time without anything to do. How long do you think that I will let that go on? Before the idle guy can smell a rat, I'll be telling my boss that we have one too many people. No boss will challenge that statement; each will agree instantly to my letting one go. So I will shed this poor devil I defrocked because he was man enough not to do the same thing to his men. Now I have an excuse for my own frustrations in that I'm carrying a double load. Now I can stay busy doing what the dismissed man should have been allowed to do, and I don't have to wrap myself around the tasks that I really should be doing, but found difficult. How long it will take for my boss to see through this situation will be determined by how much he has to reach down to stay busy himself.

Defrocking at the lower and middle management levels does not make big waves in any sizeable outfit, but when it happens at or near the top, the drowning of a big shot brings a crowd to the edge of the pool. Both the man's boss and the guy just under him will be there as very interested parties. Mouth to mouth resuscitation will not occur to either, for they aren't there to save a life. The rest of the crowd will be watching these two guys and won't so much as throw in an inner tube if they are not given the word. Twice in twenty years I have seen a senior vice president, caught between an executive vice president and a scheming guy below, defrocked of his job as completely as any chicken you have ever seen plucked. Each time, the executive vice president started taking all the meat out of the victim's job. Not being a complete patsy, the senior V.P. squawked mildly, only to end up being told to confine his major efforts to certain areas, the responsibility for which rested with his main assistant. Being too honorable to strip the man below, Mr. Senior V.P. started to sit on his hands. In a matter of months, the executive vice president was talking to the president about this unproductive soul on the payroll at the top level. Out went the defrocked man in both cases, and the guy below got promoted before the ink was dry on his boss's resignation. While defrocking is usually accidental down the line, it is mostly engineered way up top, in which case, no job disappears, just a particular guy.

Pardon me for leaving the main subject at this point, but there will be no better place than right here to dwell on the "Pistol Repeat" aspects of life in a big company. Everybody watches the "Pistol Petes" of this world, whether they are clowning around on the basketball court or making the three-ring sign in a beer commercial. Everyone wants to see what frantic antic Pete will pull off next. The "Petes" are harmless, for the most part, because they are always out in the open, but not so with the Pistol Repeats, who function underneath the surface of corporate life with the calm intrigue of a Charles De Gaulle or the phantom photoplay of a Henry Kissinger. While Pete is darting around the corporate pool on one ski, Repeat is snorkeling below his own platform, scraping off barnacles, for the record, but mainly on the lookout for sharks. He needs no new tricks for killing, just new victims. In the life-and-death struggle for corporate power, Repeat will use the same deadly weapon over and over, while Pete will try to drum up some new survival kit, only to lose his own life. In the high-level example given above, defrock number two was pulled off by an executive V.P., who was the man who got promoted in defrock number one. Show a corporate big shot a method of homicide that works, and he'll roll it out on a repeat basis as long as he is in power. He doesn't need a variety of methods to get rid of the sharks beneath his platform; a single tried and true way plus a killer instinct will do. As has been shown, ex rating and funnelling are two other extremely effective ways of killing off the career of an underling, and while I have not discussed in detail, any boss can execute a person below him by deliberately giving top management a false picture of the worth of the man being praised. Every boss is a relay station for information about the people who work for him. It is easy to make sure that the people up above receive a distorted idea about any man's true worth; that is to say that a man can be killed by the "poison" fed to a third party by a big shot in a murderous mood.

Back to defrocking, which is a very lethal way to dispose of a shark, real or imaginary. Take away his duties from which come his bite, and his teeth fall out. Watch a pro in action. On the eve of battle, my outfit got a new assistant division commander with a wealth of fighting experience. Our commanding general knew the bang of blank shells in the Louisiana maneuvers but had never heard a shot fired in anger. The very presence of this new combat-tested general frightened the top guy so badly that he took action at once to strip the new arrival of his duties. Fresh from a decorated hero's performance at the Anzio beachhead in Italy, the poor guy was assigned to a regimental headquarters as an observer, as our brand-new outfit lost its virginity to the German panzers. The most experienced, capable man we had was without a duty to perform, as green American boys risked their lives that day. Why? Simply because the man in charge looked upon the new general as a threat to his own position and decided to take the uniform off his back by denying him a single duty. During that division's seven months of hard fighting, no job with teeth was ever given that backup general.

Every corporate tiger has to be careful not to become a shark. Top management sees itself as tough enough to live with a tiger whose teeth are not big. Sure, tigers scratch, but they are not too much of a death threat, and bosses like their spirit. But sharks are an entirely different matter—they scare the living hell out of higher authority, for sharks can mortally wound in one bite. Let's look at some of the hormones that can turn a useful tiger into a savage shark overnight in the mind of his boss. As with the backup general, experience and the demonstrated capacity to perform can give a man bigger teeth than top management wants him to have. Another tooth enlarger is leadership to a high degree; to a boss who has trouble maintaining a following, a born leader has fangs. A tiger with a dynamic personality will be a shark overnight, if he doesn't play it down. But the shark-breeding hormone most feared is great grass-roots popularity; leaders without it feel a decided lack of armor against the teeth of those who do. Can you believe that having one or more of these great assets can actually decrease a man's worth in the eyes of his bosses? If you can't, Pistol Repeat will have your piscatorial carcass mounted over his mantle before you ever get the chance to show him that your gums are wrapped around small teeth. By defrocking you of your duties, he can remove all your talent from underneath his platform, making it impossible for you to pose a threat to him in any way.

This is why I always studied my boss's previous career with much interest and tried very hard to measure his strengths accurately. The first was done to know what kind of "repeating" weapon he had. If I was ever to incur his wrath, I wanted to know what kind of blow to brace for. The second was pursued to get a set of limits for my own exhibited strengths. I could not afford to show more ability than he, be more personable than he, outstrip him in popularity, or show more courage, unless I was willing to face his Pistol Repeat death device. He may or may not use defrocking to put me out of business, but death by any other devious dose will be no less final.

19

FAR OUT BREEDING

INBREEDING IS THOUGHT to produce bleeders in corporate life as does incest in families. Like the sires of a clan, top management in a company believes with a passion in the introduction of new genes into the blood stream of the outfit. By so doing, leadership expects to magnify the strength of its own stock through crossbreeding with another strong line of animal flesh. Its intent is noble and its desires very valid, for too many people cast in the same mold can rob a company of variety of thought, if not coagulation of blood. But unfortunately, the pedigrees of people are nowhere near as exactly documented as are those in livestock lineage, making it quite risky to take on a piece of horseflesh from outside one's own domain. In addition, stall control is easy in the domesticated beast world, giving breeders full command over which male animal mates with which female. Not so in the hopefully O.K. Corral of a big company, where it is impossible to know who is in bed with whom. It's easy to see how well-planned steps to strengthen blood in a big company can turn out as transfusion misfires, putting stale water in the veins of the business.

Any search outside for new blood is fraught with danger. Being most careful, with or without professional "head hunter" help, is no assurance that a company will not come up with somebody else's ghost, loosed into the air, armed with a set of forged papers making him look like a colt named Hell To Breakfast, out of a mare called Dragon's Delight, by a stud dubbed Burning Bright. For a few grand in the form of a fee to some brain broker, top management crossbreeds with confidence, only to find out it now has a new cross to bear. If by some miracle the company could wring out every drop of this horse's blood and inject one hundred cubic centimeters each into its existing managers, it would still need to increase its supply of iron to ward off an outbreak of anemia. Going outside the company's own four walls in search of new red blood is not always a good move, and many companies have begun to move management men more freely within their own confines to create the effect of crossbreeding without the risk of picking up somebody else's docile donkey.

Not of much less concern than the poor quality of outside blood is the undesirable fact that top management turns its back on its own team when it shops afield for talent. The guys who have been spoon fed by management and not allowed the correct vitamins and minerals to develop their own blood properly will have enough energy to scream bloody murder when the company deserts them and goes outside to fill a big job. Therefore, it is much more attractive to management to promote from within, which also gives a push to freer switches of executives from one area of a company to another, with little regard for background or experience. Top management bills this as a great new concept of manpower movement growing out of its having such a flexible breed of modern managers. However, under closer scrutiny, it shows up for what it really is: "far out breeding" to cover the bases without having to look outside. Many a top manager has his fingers crossed today, waiting for some totally inexperienced Johnny to prove that he can run a department in which he has given not one day of previous service.

If you recall my own tour of duty as a mutual fund sales big wig, you will see the fallacy in far out breeding. My concept of a mutual fund was a joint bank account with one's wife, so maybe the practice shouldn't be criticized for such an obvious mistake. With me, it was way out breeding, but even when the assignment makes a lot more sense than mine, there is still the chance that a fine manager in one area will be a fish-out-of-water in a strange camp. I admire top managers who are willing to stake the future of a big job on an unknown quantity, as well as those men who are sure enough of their abilities to tackle strange duties, but both parties to far out breeding, management and man, should examine their motives in such a situation. Each should try to avoid a complete mismatch, but like me, hard chargers will believe that "flexibility" pitch put out by management frantic to fill a job, and will latch on to any carrot put before them.

Suppose you were a forty-year-old lawyer about three layers from the top of the legal department in your company, whose fine reputation had been built handling customer complaints with a rare record of goodwill at reasonable cost. Sitting comfortably in your office, basking in your latest skillful injection of tranquilizing serum into an upset member of the public, you are snapped out of your glory sleep by a Mr. Big who is there to do a little pick-and-shovel work for the top man. He praises the way you have handled the public and wants to know how you feel about your future, with great emphasis on whether or not you are flexible. Under such a setup, the most rigid man in captivity will declare his nimbleness. As soon as you vow to keep an open mind about your future (who wouldn't?), the big shot turns off his radar and disappears as quickly as he came. Very soon—two days is normal—you are called to the chief executive's office and offered the job of vice president for public relations. Here's the way you are spoken to: "Eagle, you have a great future as a lawyer, but you know progress is slow in the law department due to the presence of so many good men. You can feather your nest faster if you will jump over to public relations and take advantage of your ability to get along with the public. You're a flexible guy who can move around in this company, and we want you to run the department that you know needs a strong man badly." Under such coaxing, Fanny Hill would enter a convent. Could you be objective about yourself? I sure as blazes couldn't.

In this modern world of increased regulations, tax loopholes, and rising conflict, "legal eagles" are held in great respect by management men who so often have to be bailed out of some mess. Top management in many outfits would like to crossbreed lawyers with general management people. When they try it, they must use an already trained lawyer, for to do it the other way would take forever. But turning a legal eagle into a "bossy boxer" just may put too much demand on the strain of either animal for a successful crossbreeding. What to do with a "beaten beagle" or a "flossy flamingo" could become a problem. In case you do end up with some genetic misfire, you might want to weep with a certain company that put a lawyer in charge of sales. By the time that beaten beagle got through smelling around for a fireplug to suit his fancy, revenues had shrunk to peanut size. After sending him to Denmark to try to turn him back into a lawyer, the company finally had to give up and put him out to permanent pasture. He's somewhere out there now, making eyes at Ferdinand the bull, hoping to get some pleasure out of his altered condition. Lawyer, know thyself, before you get talked away from your own turf.

For that matter, every management man should know something about the ground underneath his feet. Far out breeding can add ignorance to the already deadly effects of inbreeding and confuse the people who take these far-out assignments, as well as baffle those who have to work under leadership devoid of basic knowledge. Instead of new ideas coming from the new brain grafted onto the worn-out department, the befuddled man involved tightens up out of fear. He has to dig like crazy just to keep up with simple things and finds that new thoughts cannot be born out of a brain that contains no frame of reference for the wisdom of the past in that department. Speaking of the ground beneath one's feet, have you ever seen a city kid try to make his way across a chicken yard? Only a country kid knows to carry his shoes, for it is so simple to wash feet and so hard to clean shoes. Without that frame of reference, the city kid will never be comfortable on that ground. When far out breeding puts a man on totally unfamiliar sod, the bright new ideas so sought by management may not put in an appearance. If that city kid is put in charge of that chicken yard, he'll never give a thought to the chickens or the eggs until he learns to shuck his shoes.

I have a friend who was an excellent home mortgage man in a big bank. Like every other big outfit today, his bank worked on a five-year planning cycle. Every year, my friend would tell me how happy he was when top management praised him so highly for his plans. One day, he had his visit from the pick-and-shovel guy who laid it on thick about the mortgage man being the best planner in the entire company. Before he knew what hit him, my friend had declared himself the most open-minded man around and staked a claim on flexibility that made Dunninger look as if he had a one-track mind. When he told me about this visit, I wanted to know what he would do if they asked him to take a job far removed from his field. He broke out into a cold sweat just thinking about it, but when the offer came to become a full vice president for total bank planning, he could no more say no than give up breathing. How I wish the story had a happy end, but if that bank didn't have a permanent pasture before, it has one now, including a section for little square stones with writing on them.

The chief executive is in charge of breeding and cross-breeding in any company. He has to use everything from artificial insemination to adoption of somebody else's orphans to come anywhere near filling the needs of the moment for temporary manpower to nurture the everlasting life of his particular corporate body. God will forgive him for his mistakes, for he has no more than this old verse from the dim, distant past to guide him:

What do you do when the well runs dry?
Dip a tear from an elephant's eye.
What do you do when the meat comes in?
Sit in the corner with a greasy chin.

As this verse implies, it is feast or famine in good manpower in most companies. Mr. Big has to live with the rigors of far out breeding when the well runs dry and suffer the loss of good men to other companies when the meat comes in. It's better, sometimes, to struggle along with an empty bucket than to ruin a piece of top sirloin in a meat grinder.

20

LEAPFROGGING

UNLESS YOU ARE the top guy in your company, your base of power is subject to the whims of men who sit at higher levels of corporate glory than you do. Each of those men has his own special brand of mentality, causing you to move through life mumbling to yourself, "Look at the head on that one." Each boss you have will defy you to predict his actions or reactions with any degree of consistent accuracy, so you will never learn how to figure him out. Being predictable in the eyes of one's troops is a sign of weakness to most leaders, and they would rather risk being hated for changing a stand than being admired for hanging on to fixed opinions. Those who never change their minds will end up having their rights to decide stolen by the guys below who have learned to bank on the fixed positions of their leaders. By being inconsistent, a leader can make it unhealthy for men below to take things upon themselves on the assumption that the boss will do business this time just as he has in the past on a particular issue. Relying on his boss not to change his mind can be deadly poison to a young manager's budding career.

If you can't stake your own position on the mind of your boss, where, upon that sterling leader, are you to hang your hat of personal conviction? How about the heart? While a boss's mind may have to swing back and forth to keep his skin intact, he can still be given credit for having his heart in the right place. So many times, after being slapped down, I have heard these words, "Don't be mad at Joe for changing his stand. He's not vicious; he had to do it." In other words, Joe's heart is located where it should be, but he cannot use it to influence his own mind. Outside pressures are too great for Joe to hang on to a previous stand, even though his head and his heart tell him he was right in the first place. Yet I was supposed to develop some loyalty to Joe and to support him, with no more to go on than his wind-blown mind and properly located heart. To hell with the hearts of my bosses; I learned early that there was no connecting rod from heart to brain in the mechanical robots who manage big business. So where do you turn to find enough consistency in a boss to inspire your loyalty, a much sought-after strength in yourself as well as a mark of teamwork in a boss's eyes? How about the abdomen? Is that a good place to find rocklike traits upon which to rely or to stake your loyalty to a boss? While women have been saying for years that the way to a man's heart is through his stomach, getting there by that or any other route will only take one to a dead end. No matter how you get to the heart, it is still not connected to the brain.

After giving up on the brain and heart, I passed right by the stomach and tried the feet. It seemed logical that every man would want his feet planted on some kind of solid ground and that his feet would give me a clue to where he stood on most things of value. Forget it; the average manager has his feet on a bed of hot coals and at best dances to whatever tune is drifting down from higher up. When it comes to developing loyalty to a boss, throw out the head, the heart, the guts, and the feet. You'll never be able to figure them out. But there's one hope left: his rear end. Every big shot you ever meet will be consistent in one thing; he'll want his rear end catered to, regardless of what's going on in his mind and heart or what kind of fire is burning in his gut or under his feet.

Every boss I ever had expected homage out of me. While such terms as brown-nosing and ass-kissing are more often heard in the army than in business, the fact remains that corporate bosses do spend time bent in a position to be kissed, with their trousers at half-mast. They are consistently ready for the outward show of respect that most men trying to climb the ladder in a company are prone to give. The bent-over, ass-above-tea-kettle stance for being kissed is, in itself, an unmoving position—a model of constancy. From that jack-knifed posture, it is not possible to think, show compassion, eat, or run; they can only appreciate having their rears balmed in some fashion. Kiss me, kiss me, eight to the bow-down.

So what's this consistency by bosses who want to be kissed got to do with loyalty? Absolutely nothing, but the sense of power that comes from having his ass kissed is far more exciting to a boss than devotion in any other form. Not being able to fight his way through Queen Elizabeth's many skirts to get to her ass, Sir Walter Raleigh showed his good intentions by covering up the mud in her path with his coat, thereby paving his way to knighthood by her hand. The Queen's sense of power was so titillated by Sir Walter's presence that she forbad him to leave England. It made much more sense to Bess to use less charming courtiers to tackle the raging seas and settle the New World than to give up Raleigh, who would bathe her butt in olive oil at the drop of her ruffled, feathery petticoats. While power is many times its own reward, it is more often a source of wounds to the person who bears its burdens. Queen Elizabeth found this fact out as Protestants and Catholics alike tried their best to bring her down. They plagued her mind with treachery, hardened her heart with hate, plotted poisonings for her stomach, and chafed her rear end with deceit. None of these wounds could she lick herself. History can hardly blame her for wanting Raleigh around to at least soothe her roughed-up tail.

And so it is in big business. Bosses get burned by bigger bosses from their heads to their toes and yearn for some balm of Gilead from the troops below. If a boss, blistered from above, can't get homage from below, he feels completely powerless. That's why the brown-nosers and ass-kissers of this world will never be put out of business. In fact, there will always be a premium on their services. Therefore, early in my career, it became necessary to adopt some kind of philosophy about how I should react to the basic fact that the most important part of my boss's body was his ass, as far as my own progress was concerned. I could not rely on his head, his heart, his guts, or his feet, but I could be sure of his consistent support, if I kissed his ass around the block as an outward show of my devotion to his kind, unselfish leadership. At the time, television chortled at me to "double my pleasure, double my fun" by chewing on a special brand of chewing gum. I often wondered if I might get the same effect by making like a Frenchman and kissing my bosses on both cheeks. In my final decision as to what to do about kissing asses, I gravitated toward leapfrogging to cut my pleasure in half, rather than to run it up.

As I made my entry into management, I looked in front of me at the men who held the seats of power over mine. Knowing that my progress would be geared to how I handled them, rather than the other way around, I yearned to hold my relationships with them to benign aloofness in an effort to move up without having to alter my own personality. It was a shock to see those guys lined up in order of rank, bent over, pants in the ready position, mooning for my new and different kisses. First I tried to put my palm on their butts so I could kiss the back of my hand, but that kind of aloofness got me absolutely nowhere. I started looking around for puddles to help people over, in lieu of kissing, but puddle jumping will not lead one to a big splash in the big pool of corporate affairs. Whether I liked it or not, I had to face up to kissing certain asses if I was to get a hold on some power of my own. That's when I started leapfrogging over every other boss in line above me, to cut my distaste for the task in half.

If one is going to play this game, he may as well be as scientific as possible. With an even number of bosses above me, it made no difference whether I started up the line with a kiss or a leap, but if the number was odd, I could come out better by beginning with a leap. Lucky me, I usually had an odd number above me, so I was able to go through my career kissing less than half the total asses out in front of me. But I kid you not, I couldn't dare take the risk of kissing any less. Two bosses in a row who didn't care if I sank or swam were too great a threat to my own personal safety. If one boss had doubts about my loyalty, I wanted to be sure that the one above him did not. Here's where the rear-end constancy of bosses comes in handy. If I kissed a man's ass, I could bank on his thinking I was loyal. Catering to a man's head, heart, guts, or feet will not make him appreciate you one bit in the clutch, but bending down to lap his wounded tail will give him a secure feeling about your devotion in all matters. Doesn't it give you a warm feeling to know that the only connecting rod to a man's brain from the rest of his body is hooked up to his butt? If I wanted to yank on the mind of a boss, I had to kiss his ass to find the handle on the end of the rod.

Obviously, there could be no real loyalty on my part to any of my bosses. The ones being kissed were not being loved, and the ones being leaped were not being catered to at all. So what? Each of them was as temporary in the overall scheme of things as I was. Yet I did have mankind's universal urge to be loyal to something, so I reviewed the list of things to which I had previously pledged allegiance. Included were my country, the flag, my church, at least two honor codes, and my wife. My wife was the only human being that I had ever pledged an ounce of my blood to support. That's when it hit me: the everlasting corporate body was the thing to which I owed my loyalty as far as my

business life was concerned. Only in it could I find any consistency of head, heart, guts, and feet, and it would never
bare its ass for me to kiss. If I was good to it, the everlasting
corporate body would be good to me, no matter which fickle
human beings sat in seats of power bigger than mine. That's
when I decided to cater to management to the least degree
possible, while staying afloat by pulling just enough strings or
kissing the minimum requirement of rear ends. I made it for
quite a spell, but when the strings ran out and the butts got
too salty, I had to pack it in.

Thank God for the everlasting corporate body. It sustained this temporary little piece of humanity to a handsome
level of personal reward and gave me and my family the foundation for a good life. It had nothing to do with the asses I
had to kiss, the leapfrogging I elected to do, or any other
corporate games I saw fit to play. Its mission was, and still
is, perfectly aboveboard, and being everlasting, it will get
to its goals, regardless of what petty little games we leaders
inflict upon it. Maybe I could have served it better by giving
up my yearning for aloofness to butter every butt in sight,
but I was just not built that way. If you aren't either, try leapfrogging. It sure as blazes beats kissing them all.

21

BUFFERING

A BUFFER LESSENS, absorbs, or protects against the shock of an impact. It's only natural to want a buffer between you and anything bad. I like shock absorbers to help protect me and mine from bad odors, bad tastes, bad scenes, and bad people. And furthermore, I like to use my own definition of what's bad; seldom do I accept something as good for me just because mama or papa or some big boss says it is. This need to be buffered against evil as I see it through my own eyes started in my life long before I gave one thought to big business. In the beginning, as well as later while employed, some threats to my peace of mind were very real, while some were purely images of fear growing out of trumped-up doubts. However, in or out of business, anything I saw as bad was real enough, and gave birth to "buffering," my defense against whatever I saw as a threat. By being alert to things that I considered dangerous, by setting up buffers for protection before impact, and by being willing to miss some thrills as the result of being too careful, I know that I was able to avoid a lot of heartache.

In corporate life, I built walls between me and a variety of dangers. For instance, I saw the social trap that one's family can get rolled into as an outgrowth of business obligations as a bad deal. My first act of buffering, when I entered the home office, was to move as far away from the executive population center in my company as I could get. When we headed for Long Island, instead of Fairfield County, Connecticut, where every big shot in the sales department lived, people in the know said that my future was impaired. So what, I wanted myself and my family buffered against the social life up there, no matter what the cost. Distance and travel time make a great shield when one is turning down invitations to parties at the boss's house. Now that I'm retired, the politicians can put a bridge over Long Island Sound from some place in Nassau County to New England any time they wish, but I'm surely glad they didn't break down my buffer while I still needed it. I'm equally pleased that I was the first guy living on the wrong side of the Sound who got to be an executive officer in the sales department.

I cannot speak for your industry, but the life insurance business is loaded with trade associations and other organizations like no business I know. If you let yourself get involved to the degree possible, you would be up to your ears in outside activities before you know it. I had gotten my belly full of this aspect at the local level in my early days in the field, so I determined to buffer against it as I entered the national scene. I saw excessive movement into industry affairs as an inroad on my business time and a drain on the company's resources, not to mention an adverse effect on the energy that I much preferred to pour into pursuits unrelated to business. My buffer was to make it clear to top management that all such industry jazz was not my cup of tea. The powers that be will never send out a delegate to a convention nor put a man on an outside committee unless he shows some real interest in what's going on. Nothing was lost to the industry or by the company as a result of my not being wrapped up in these things, but I do wish to make it clear that I lost personally by excluding myself. I missed some thrilling exposure to some very exciting people both in and out of our business. If you engage in buffering, be prepared to give up some nice things as the price you must pay for building a fence of your own design around your person.

I saw certain people as bad for a wide set of reasons. I am threatened by men who lie, men who forget what they tell you, men who imply one thing and do another, men who breed clashes between others to further their own causes, and men who pull a Pontius Pilate in the face of a tough choice. Without buffers, one can be killed by such guys. So in all matters involving men who might fit one of these descriptions, I always put my position on paper and put copies in enough files, to make sure that one would be in the right hands if I ever needed a buffer to ward off the effects of some guy's lying, chickening out, talking out of school, or conveniently forgetting. It's sad to know that you have to work like that to protect yourself, but it's a must when dealing with some people. Memos to the file are common practice for safety's sake; I much preferred to nail things down by memos to living, breathing people, copying the guy I didn't trust. It's much more effective this way, even if the man's feathers get ruffled. Pardon my language, but as the old saying goes, "He will think twice before he screws the dog," thereby increasing the strength of my buffer.

I hate deals made on trains and planes and golf courses because they will not stand up under a close look by the total company. To me, such deals are threats to good business practices and are almost never done with the whole outfit in mind. Otherwise, why would the people involved literally sneak off to do the deed? There can be but one answer; they do not want any opposing voice around. I buffered myself against this practice by staying away from my business associates when traveling and by playing my golf with people outside my company. No one could get me to talk business in a restricted setup; I insisted on being in somebody's office, where men who might be against the issue could be brought in. When Castro came up from Cuba with chickens on his plane, it was not the first nor the last time that eggs got laid at thirty thousand feet. Business tycoons were doing it long before Fidel flew in and still are.

Aware of my need for shock-resisting barriers around me, I never had an adverse reaction when other people threw up buffers to soften my impact upon them. Managing me could hardly head up any man's happiness list, and many of my bosses built circular defenses of some sort to keep me out of their hair. There was one poor guy who would scream, "Circle the wagons," just meeting me in the hall. To him, I was a hostile influence at best, not without reason in his mind, I'm sure. He was my immediate boss longer than any one man, but he was never relaxed when I was around. All those years, I was sitting outside his circle of wagons smoking a pipe of peace, but he thought I was poisoning my arrows and honing my tomahawk in preparation for some wild Comanche charge. Rather than irritating, I found this situation amusing, even helpful. While I was free to roam the range, he was a prisoner within his own wagons. While I was eating pleasant pheasant with all the guys and gals in his department, he was cramming down crummy crow, dished up by the same people. They felt secure with me and not with him. In medicinal terms, buffers are supposed to ease headaches; the ones that boss threw up against me were causing his head to throb. Being more of a warrior than a medicine man, I left him to his own unfriendly circle.

One way for a big shot to buffer himself against another manager is to keep at least one other man between himself and the guy with whom he wants no contact. During my entire service as a manager at the home office level, a single individual was the top boss. He promoted me seven times, but there were always four men between him and me. The thickness of the buffer was never less than four bodies. While I cannot swear to the intentional or unintentional aspects of this happening, the fact remains that the four bodies were there—buffering by chance or design made no difference. Not once did that man discuss an idea of mine with me in

person; he would have meeting after meeting on something
that I had started, but always with the four buffer guys, with
me absent. I had lots of laughs with some of the in-between
guys about the big boss's obvious need to be sealed off from
me when my ideas were being weighed. Several said they
thought it had something to do with the top man's not wanting too much knowledge on the subject present in the mind
of one man. My presence would give Mr. Big a feeling of lost
power. One man said that our leader did not like to end a
meeting feeling like he knew less on a matter than any man
in the room, that it wasn't just me being buffered, it was my
thorough knowledge on the particular subject. Knowing that
I would not let him break up the meeting feeling superior
on my idea, the chief just ruled me out. God bless him for
knowing me so well and reducing the possibility of friction
between us.

Few men have had any more training than I have had
in the old adage, "A good offense is the best defense." Athle-
tics teach this to every kid in America, and around the sand
box, make-believe war games at West Point, we cadets were
taught to "attack, attack" as a way to save lives. In modern
two-platoon football, it is impossible to win without scoring,
and even such gentle games as tennis and golf place great
emphasis on being aggressive. From pocket pool to poker, no
one favors the attack any more than I. Having found that
success as a temporary human being, swept up in the everlasting life of a corporation, has as much to do with good
defenses as with the attack, I can see how the youth of today
fear the Establishment so much more than did the young of
my day. Ever since "my generation" whipped Hitler and
came home, it has been assaulting the everlasting corporate
body, drawing back a bloody nub ninety-nine percent of the
time, and bitching about its frustrations to the wife and kids
over the dining table. Those kids are now today's young
people and they do not want the big business part of the

Establishment to thwart their aggressive urges as it did those of their dads.

In order not to be bamboozled by big business, many of these youths are claiming a lack of drive and desire as a buffer against having their aggression blunted by the ever-lasting corporate body. They bill themselves as being reluctant to engage in something where aggressiveness is going to be a requirement, but they consider themselves a failure if they don't "score" by the second date. They buffer against business by latching on to whichever political candidate appears to be most aggressive in his promises to clip the wings of corporations, never considering that most of his campaign money is coming from the very companies whose wings he is promising to nip. They head for a commune in an Alfa Romeo and kill themselves at ninety miles an hour on the way there. Don't tell me they don't have drive and desire. They have it to the highest degree in history, and they don't want it nipped in the bud by the Establishment, be it business, government, or otherwise. The easiest buffer against anything is not to get involved, and many are using noninvolvement against business today.

But the Establishment is going to get them, for three score and ten years is a long time to dangle from a single thread of life without touching down somewhere. Upon touching down, the youth of all ages will find that life is a mixture of attack and defense and that neither aggression nor the lack of it is a virtue in and of itself. A night spent in the woods to get away from it all will usually find one needing a buffer against red bugs and mosquitoes, if not a skunk. Try the beach on a bright hot day. Until you have been in the sun for some trial period, you'll need a buffer of suntan oil. So whether one uses his aggressiveness to run to something or away from it, he'll need to be aware of the dangers and ever mindful of the role that buffers must play in his life. Buffering is the only antidote for shock and its impact, past, present, or future, in business or without. Don't run, tiger. Size

up the jungle wherever you touch down and attack with passion, but exercise some care in the process to buffer both
real and imaginary threats. My generation is your Establishment. Can you manage so well that your generation will not
be some kind of millstone around the neck of your offspring?
Or will your own flesh and blood need to be buffered against
you?

22

DULL SKULLERY

THE MOST WONDERFUL mind in the world is not big enough to make much of an impression around a big company. The total knowledge stored up in a giant corporation dwarfs any one mind that comes along. Therefore, no single person's death or departure ever hurts a company very much. Any man's brain is a "pea brain" compared to the wealth of mental capacity wrapped up in the crowd. On the other hand, that wealth of brain power spread all over the place makes it possible for a truly dull skull to flourish. A man can be dumb, dumb, dumb, when it comes to his own brain, but he can work wonders by the art of scraping together a pile of brains from several people. In fact, this need to accumulate thought power from a wide source makes the dumb guy look like a great team man. Top management would much rather deal with a person who can pile up brains from a group than with a man who has a sizeable supply in his one skull. "Dull skullery" is faked dumbness on the part of a really smart guy to keep from posing a threat to higher management in the brain power department.

We'll take a look at how one practices dull skullery later, but first let's go inside some sure-enough dull skulls sitting on the shoulders of some high-ranking business executives who did all right in spite of their limited mentalities. While on the phone with a certain guy, I always heard a little low-pitched ticking sound. When hooked up with other people, I never heard just that same extra tone. One day, I was discussing this man's rather slow mental reaction time with another person, who said, "That guy's so dumb that my phone picks up mechanical tones of a strange nature when I talk to him." I have seen many men whose wheels did turn when they thought, but this is the only one I met whose mechanical mental processes could actually be heard, at least on the phone. A dog with sensitive ears in that man's house would have lost his mind, but few cats around the company ever heard the tick. Being a good hand at sweeping together brain power when he needed it, he was able to reap the benefits from dull skullery without effort. Lucky is the truly dull skull who does have the ounce of wisdom to draw on the total brain power lying around the corporate body. Such a man can go far.

Slow readers are so much in evidence among high-level executives that I'll speak to them as a category and not single out an example. While being a slow reader may not be a sure sign of low brain power, it can have a ravaging effect on one's peace of mind in high places. If two executives get the same piece of written dope at the exact same time, each's ability to react quickly is purely a function of reading time. Suppose I'm a slow reader and I get a twenty-page report at the same time my boss does, and he's a quick gulper of the written word. If my "reading-lag time" on this much material is one day, compared to my boss, I can be much embarrassed if some guy calls a meeting to dig into that report before my slow reading ability has time to bring me up to date. It's a dumb, dumb, dumb manager who doesn't take this into account in setting up meetings in which he wants to put over some point. If he calls such a session before the main decision guy has time to read, what chance does he have to get what he wants?

When I found out that a particular big shot was a slow reader, I could either protect him or hurt him. If I wanted to

keep him from looking dumb, I could give him advance copies of papers with lead time to match his reading-lag time. By
so doing, I could bring him into a meeting on a par with the
crowd, as far as knowing what was on paper was concerned.
If I wanted to kill him, I would shove a piece of paper into his
hand as we entered the meeting room and watch him
squirm. A three-sentence memo can bring on panic in such a
situation, for slow readers are even slower under pressure.
You can rest assured that this session will end with nothing
being decided, for Mr. Slow Reader will cloud up and rain.
The game will be called for wet grounds. When I wasn't
ready to go to bat, I could bring about a postponement by
manipulating the slow reader.

Lucky is the manager who can scan a raft of material
and still get the drift. Men with dull skulls cannot scan at all.
They have to pore and pore over everything they look at, but
by doing just that, many take the time to absorb all the facts
they need to know. My hat's off to them, for they make up
for their lack of quickness by sheer guts. Being a fast reader,
I held slow ones in contempt, but that didn't keep two or
three genuine dull skulls from going by me on the corporate
racetrack as if I was standing still. I enjoyed having my ordinary brain made to look more bright due to those rather limited ones drifting about in high places, but I found out that
the height of the lamppost has more to do with how far a light
can be seen from the ground than does its wattage. In the
final showdown, top management is the engineer who
decides on the height of the poles from which will shine all
the light bulbs in the outfit. A fifty watter who has the knack
of borrowing juice from other bulbs is more likely to climb a
higher pole than a three hundred watter who gets a reflector
and blinds his bosses. Top management does not wish to be
bedazzled from below by brains, and many smart guys use
the art of dull skullery to make their way farther up the pole.

I discovered dull skullery before I got involved in management. Being more of a mathematician than any other

variety of student, I sought out prospects for the sale of insurance who had numbers in their backgrounds. Engineers were particularly attractive prospects for me. Armed with my slide rule, pad, and multicolored pencil, I would descend on one like an atomic scientist planning the next underground explosion. After using the slip stick like a scalpel to open up his heart to more life insurance, I found myself on the way out the door with no sale. I began to wonder whether or not math was an exact science. One night, my dauber was so down that I left my tools in the car. First, I had to borrow a pencil, which gave him a chance to show off his most expensive job and feel dominant in our relationship. I multiplied seven times seven and got forty-eight. By then, he owned me, but felt sorry for me, too. He took some life insurance away from me, and I went home knowing the power of having a dull skull. But, brother, the hardest thing I have ever had to do in my life is to act dumb. I should say "dumber," for every man is dumb when his brain is stacked up beside the accumulation of smarts in the everlasting corporate body.

All through school, youngsters are pushed to show their brains. As early as junior high, medals are passed out for everything from cooking to chemistry. High school sees its salutatorian and its valedictorian, not to mention its scholarships to college. College has its Phi Beta Kappa, its cum this, and cum that. How can any man or woman, worth his or her salt, go on in life without trying to strut his mental stuff? It's difficult not to, and it's a good thing that most people enter some field where showing off their mind's power is not a threat to their progress. But the man or woman who enters the general management level of a big company had better pay some attention as to how mentally sharp not to be. If one has my distaste for the very thought of acting dumber than he is, he should specialize, not generalize. Business needs a huge supply of people who can manage in a general sense, and there is gold to be mined in them thar hills. Smart guy, get out your pan and start panning; just make sure you use a rusty-looking utensil which will not reflect strongly enough to give away the location of your lode.

The best mind we had in the sales department of my company suffered from its own constant glitter. The human being in whom it resided couldn't understand why so many other managers turned off completely when he got involved with them in anything mentally challenging. He would study the law before he consulted the lawyers, bone up on mortality before he talked to the underwriters, and study computers before he dealt with the electronics people. Can you blame the specialists for clamming up when dealing with a general type manager who was likely to know more about their field than they did themselves? Oh, you say you understand that clearly? Then you'll easily see why a smart all-around manager is just as much of a threat to his cohorts among the other generalists, particularly the ones in charge. If our smart guy had not learned how to dull skull it, he would have never become effective.

Top management is reluctant to have too many things filtering up from below which show more original thinking than it could have generated itself. As leadership works its way to the top of a company, it builds the type of outfit over which it wants to preside. It's not easy to go for changes which might tend to throw out the things it used to gain the seat of power. Too much new thinking will not be welcome to the guys on top, and any mind that puts out an oversupply will suffer for it. Therefore, many with fine minds parcel out their brains in order not to appear too bright. Such men recognize the fact that top management intends to wield the final scoop into the overall mentality of the everlasting corporate body on any big project and that the men in charge are not likely to pile up brain power in excess of their own comprehension. By the use of dull skullery, these smart guys play down their own brain waves and help top management scrape up just what thoughts it needs at the moment. The big guys' brains don't get threatened, and the smart guys wait in the wings for their turn at the helm. What a pity, by the time they get there, they're not so smart anymore themselves.

At least I wasn't, but for better or worse, here's how I dulled it. I usually got smart by research: nosing around into the domains of others until I put two and two together in a way to make four more of a certainty. For simplicity, let's say that I have put a great thought together from four directions that usually don't work closely with one another. I have studied the thing until I am ninety percent sure it will stand up under fire. With nothing in writing, I ask the boss to get together with me and four other guys to take a "preliminary" look at a new idea. After he sets up the meeting, I see each of the others alone to tell them everything I profess to know, which is very little, of course. In the session, the pile of brains so cleverly scraped together comes up with just what I knew it would. Mr. Big goes out of that room feeling like a king who has just gotten his castle allowance tripled for the coming year—all is right with the world. Had I hit him with my brilliance, growing out of all that digging I did, he would have been like the sultan who sent all of his wives to bed but one, only to find her out of the mood. He would have been yelling for four or five more bodies right away.

The army dull skulled it in Southeast Asia so long that it began to look like they really were dumb. Before President Kennedy was killed, General Jim Gavin was over there and made a proposal on how to cool it way back then. The politicians got him out of their hair so fast that he left the service. Cooling it wasn't top management's idea of what we ought to do. Since Gavin, the powers-that-be haven't let a man in the army say a word. I don't know whether the guys in charge over there really were dull skulls, or whether they were just playing the game for the sake of promotions, combat records, and medals, but you can count your heroes on the fingers of an arm cut off at the wrist. Top management busted more careers than it made heroes—a sorry turn of events. There surely won't be any Eisenhowers running around political conventions in any election year any time soon. Dull skullery will be with us in all walks of life until the end of time, but there are some situations where it is better to blow one's mind and hit the road than to shrink one's brain to fit the hatband of higher authority. Feet hurt when bound; brains seem more able to take it.

23

RAT RACING

WHEN MEN ARE dropped like rats, in the middle of the floor in a big company, they scurry to a safe hole somewhere to get their bearings. As lights start to shine and good odors arise, they begin to stir. Some get caught in traps and die quickly. Some are scared, but they make limited runs for bare survival, staying lean all their lives out of fright. Some luck out early on huge chunks of cheese and run back to their holes in which they hope to live on their own fat. A few stay poised at the ready, eyes wide open, waiting for the more promising rays of light or more delicate odors. These are not content with meager fare and are not yet fat enough to live on their own lard. This hungry and daring group is watching for openings leading to large tasty squares of high-grade cheese. On any signal, they dart wildly about the kitchen of the everlasting corporate body's dwelling place, frighten each other, and yearn for some semblance of order. To bring rhyme or reason out of helter-skelter "rat racing" around, top management lays out lanes, draws finish lines, and designs the trophies.

When a young manager joins a company, he expects to race at once, for the guy who hired him said he would. But his first assignment is in some hole, and he has to diddle in the dark before he finds the light to the starting line. Sooner or later, he gets the chance to run. When he does, he comes up with one of three brushes with the fickle finger of fate. He dies from a smash of hard copper wire across his neck in some trap; he tires of racing and decides to spend his life scrounging for peanuts close to his hole; he gets a taste of victory and darts for the start of the next race. Every time he runs, the three possible encounters with the fickle finger of fate stare him in the face.

Rat racing is a way of life in big business; top management cannot bear the thought of having only one man interested in a single big cheese of a job. When the men on top were journeymen, they had to race for every morsel of food they got. And besides, how can they tell whether or not a man is still full of fight if he hasn't been in a recent race? So, managers all, rough up the soles of your feet; get ready to try for traction on the linoleum. Stay between the lines, keep your eye on the target, don't nip at the hide of the starter, observe the rules, charge the finish line, winner take all, and bow down to the head rat waving the checkered flag.

As an officer of the company, I often had to fill jobs at lower levels. I always got a warm feeling from having at least two men who I thought had the talent to take over. I never wanted to be forced to pick a particular guy for the lack of another candidate. In theory, if one has two promotable men, one is able to exercise selective judgment, and the manager who has to fill a job with but one candidate is committing a cardinal sin. I could have two lousy guys to pick from, and no one would care, but having a single good man to install would get me second guessed all over the place. This rat was still running, and I was not about to foul up my own race in the main corporate kitchen by canceling the races in the pantry for which I was responsible. The rats who ultimately emerged from my domain had to be touch, tested racers, or I would find myself retired to mud—rats have no stud value. Too bad.

If I was expected to promote these road shows, just think what the competition was like in the main oval. At the big job levels in the officer ranks, top management will have two or more men running madly for each vacancy long before the slot is to be filled. Even after the head boss has made up his mind as to who will step into a big position, he will carefully stage a race to make it appear as though his choice is still open. He thereby keeps the running going for entertainment's sake, if for no other reason. We had a race at the top of the company that was a complete fakery. There was a single executive vice president locked in to succeed the retiring chief, with three years to wait. With about two years left in the career of father rat, out of nowhere comes another executive V.P., put in charge of government relations. The first guy was still in charge of all operating departments, but he began to worry about the chance that things could really change in two years. Rat racing began in earnest, and Mr. Big got some good laughs out of the ersatz contest. After the second guy was given three departments to hover over a few months later, the chosen rodent began to froth at the mouth, but he survived the faked race.

Two of my best friends came into the home office from field management on the same day I did. Like good rats, we headed for our assigned holes, not knowing we were locked in mortal combat. A ray of light was beamed into each of our darkened niches, and all three of us were coaxed toward the same racetrack. Had we refused to run, the word would have gone out that a bunch of sissy mice, not men, had been brought in and that the company had better get another crop. Being more prone to scrap, I won that particular race with laps to spare, but it was a rather hollow victory over friends. I enjoyed other races more, where the other guys didn't mean much to me as people. Brother rats were fun to beat, but special people were something else. Because of the nature of the opposition, I was pitted in a couple of races in which I refused to run. I didn't withdraw publicly, of course, but I went to the guys involved and told them that I was not in the running. We enjoyed ourselves watching top management keep score on a race that wasn't even being run.

The low birth rate in the nineteen thirties made for a shortage of rats in the corporate kitchens of American business in the fifties and early sixties, but the need may be over-supplied today. Top management set up the racing syndrome when it really had enough jobs for everybody. It could put on these races to help speed up expansion of the business, knowing that even those who came in second would get a big prize. Now, it is facing a new set of conditions; there are far fewer jobs than there are rats on the prowl, but most companies are still geared to hold such races. Also, most young rats expect to move, baby, move. So the system is now starting to bite at the rear of the older guys who set it up. After about four crisp runs in winning races, younger rats begin to feel their oats, and they want to be in charge. It's a common thing in each day's paper to see chief executives stepping aside at age forty-nine or fifty, bitten by some rat who wouldn't quit running when he was told. If room is not made at the very top for such mobile specimens, they throw their trophies back into the face of the guy who taught them to run and hit the road in search of bigger cheeses. "I've got to have move-ment," say these roving rodents, as their wanderings finance a whole new industry known as "executive search."

Whether these aggressive, hungry creatures are win-ning races in only one company or snowing the ordinary rats in many locations, there's plenty of movement all right. Unfortunately, they are leaving a string of rat pills as they catapult along. Movement being their prime concern, they seldom neaten up as they move through a company or an industry. I spent three years cleaning up after one such care-less young rat, and retirement kept me from making it a career. Compensation in excess of fifty thousand a year is too much pay for operating the sewer system for company race-tracks. To wax biblical for a moment, "I fought a few good fights, ran some spirited races, and kept the faith up to a point, but policing up the pills behind young, hell-on-wheels, easy-riding rats with no desire to clean up their own messes is not my idea of heaven." Gentlemen, clean your engines.

I am a lucky old rat. I can make it on my own. But when top management stops beaming light into its eyes, usually a rat will hunt a permanent hole as a pack rat. Being no more than spectators at the company racetrack, pack rats do not expend energy at a rapid rate anymore, but putting them out to pasture as field mice is not in the cards, for they have not the blubber to survive. Beefing up early retirement is a step in the right direction, but let's look at some numbers to see just how far away from a solution we are as a people. As rats, we're pretty well off, but as people, we have miles to go before we sleep in peace on the matter of old folks, even among managers of the everlasting corporate body. Take a guy who has run hard, won races, and hit fifty-five at a salary of thirty thousand dollars. Maybe one of business' richest retirement plans would pay him ten thousand now to step down.

Poor old rat, he's out of the race, but can't bow out. So he stays on, operating the sewer system, or doing something else just as distasteful in his eyes. It takes him about a month to realize that he's now working for twenty thousand clams— his income less what he could quit for—and he cuts back on his effort by a third. Over the next ten years, he'll be the highest-paid sewer rat in captivity. Rat racing will continue to burn up most men before age fifty-five, and few will be in the mainstream of the everlasting corporate body past that age. Instead of bitching at the system which packs them into holes and sewers, older rats would do well to thank their lucky stars for the milk of corporate kindness that keeps them on the payroll. There's an old hymn that includes the line, "Give us grace and give us glory," but it had the hereafter in mind. In corporate life, the rats race for glory and forget the need for grace. What a pity, for many sorely need it to help end their careers with dignity, after their power has waned and their glory flown.

24

IDOLATRY

IN BUSINESS, BLIND devotion is to be avoided. Managers are charged with the elimination of weakness, and blind devotion will keep people, things, and concepts around long after their cracks begin to show. Love or devotion, even though blind, is usually born out of a good relationship—a valid beginning. Time then takes its toll, and devotion puts blinders on a man or a company, making it impossible for him or it to see the present holes in the armor of the thing loved or the person revered. However, time takes a second toll, and most men and companies give up their deep attachments before blind devotion leads to ruin. On the other hand, "idolatry" is a graver threat to managers and companies. It turns an idea or a person into a god, and no one likes to kill a deity. Rather than a natural birth from a good beginning, idolatry springs from a source of power by edict backed by muscle. Mr. Strong Man says, "Thou shalt have no other gods before me," and claps his thunder, or he declares his ideas to reign over the brain children of all other managers. In the face of raw power, men are prone to light candles of worship and to keep them burning for idols.

When an idea is turned into a top priority concept and deified, it gets constant attention from the entire managing group at all levels. Anointed by top management, such an idol will never be challenged. No one will hop forward to doubt its worth, and each manager below the top will step to its theme song. I have seen faulty thinking idolized by edict, folded into the policy statement of the company, and not once openly doubted by the fallen angels inside the pearly gates of the executive suite, including me. Here's an example of what can happen. Our chief was a salesman by trade, and he built this bias into the outfit's operating policy as follows, "The sales department is not the whole company, but the whole company should be the sales department." Sounds great until you examine it closely, particularly if you're a salesman, as I was. But suppose you are a controller, an underwriter of risks, a claim payer, an investment man, or a lawyer; it will have a different ring. Outside of the sales area, it quickly begins to sound like this, "You bastards in the other departments had better not get in the way of sales in any way."

Awed by power and ordered to worship at the shrine of the chief's edict, weak managers outside of sales could default in their charge to keep the company solvent financially and vigorous in its nonsales functions. To prove his reverence for the boss's idol, a controller could let the cost of doing business rise too fast, a risk taker could take bad business to speed up sales, a claim payer could pay fraudulent claims to spawn more prospects, and a lawyer could stretch the law to help the field. In addition, what sales officer wouldn't push like crazy to gain any advantage he could? Thank the real God that this heavy leaning toward the sales side of our business house didn't throw things completely out of kilter, but worshiping the chief's idol about the sacredness of the sales department caused much friction among high level managers, which would not have arisen without the faulty manifesto written into the policy statement of the company. The chief had to reach the end of his line before the damaging demigod of his own "loyalty" to the sales arm of the company got blown to hell.

On the nonperson list of idols, long-range planning has taken over as the grand deity of all. Across the business world, it is getting a play that is unprecedented in its intensity, and my guess is that most of management's worshiping time will be wasted. I believe that top management has a guilty feeling about the accidental aspects of success and that long-range planning is its way of trying to make future triumphs look like planned victories. Leadership that has trouble seeing three months down the road is being asked to plan for five or more years. Because the operating people in most of these planning mills cannot begin to do a decent job of long-range scanning, there is a great demand for corporate planners, as one can see by watching the executive recruiting ads in any large newspaper. Since few companies have ever done much of a job in this field, the advertisers are really looking for a needle in the haystack. It takes a while to train priests, rabbis, and ministers to serve any new god, be he real or trumped-up. A guy with a secretary named Crystal was describing his weekend as he rode the Long Island Railroad to work, and a man across the aisle offered him a job. Somehow, in his dire need for a long-range planner, the eavesdropper's ears heard "crystal balling" instead of "balling Crystal."

Another cutie, high up the list of modern business idols, is using computers to make top management decisions. By draining more facts out of the machinery, it is felt that big bosses can interpret conditions more accurately and decide things more clearly. Two things make this idea a false god, in my estimation. One, it's easy to get stuff out of the machines, but getting the same stuff into the heads of managers is another kettle of fish. Two, there is hardly a manager who is managing up to the quality and the amount of his present information, and more dope will most likely make him more dopey. I don't blame top cats for wanting all that expensive hardware to grind out something more than its daily input-output chores, but earthly hot dogs and hamburgers for empty stomachs will make more sense than celestial pie-in-the-sky for vacant heads. A god the computer is not, but the guys who make them will do all they can to create the mythology that says it's so, and top management will help them.

While not a religion, mythology can help create the needed gods—the idols to satisfy. Top management can comfort itself in any tight squeeze by setting up another idol. One year's failure to cling to the god of "cost control" can be lost in the new worship of an idol called "increased productivity," which may be an even larger devil in disguise. One day's thrilling devotion to the tin god of "growth" may have to give way to the bridled idol of tomorrow's "status quo." Watch the beer commercials and you'll see what I mean. After a season of bragging about its larger bottles with the big mouths, the same company today will try to get the public to worship its small can from which you can hardly drink. An airline will serve holy communion in a spacious lounge to the tune of some drunk on a piano in the front part of a sixty-second television bit and bow down moments later to an idol suffering from claustrophobia in an intimate little nook where a jew's-harp player would be a menace. Like advertisers, top managers change idols as they change shoes. Man is very adept at setting up a ritual and conjuring up the idol to fit it.

There is one situation, however, in which man is very much like Jehovah, who first said, "There shall be no other gods before me." When a man sits on the top seat of corporate power and is worshiped by flying rats with angel wings, he proves beyond doubt that man is made in the image of God, for he, too, makes it clear that there shall be no other idols before him. While a company can make idols out of many concepts at the same moment, it can worship but one man at a time. When an outfit tries to deify more than one human being at once, the rank and file will find themselves being chosen by one side or the other to be cannon fodder for a management Armageddon. Smart rats hunt for holes and leave the entire kitchen floor to the Grand Prix of idolatry, from which but one idol can survive.

Regardless of which man makes it to corporate divinity, ordinary managers like you and me are then supposed to accept the commandments of the deified human being in power. How many times have I sat in the "sabbath school" of Mr. Big and heard these words, "You can say anything you wish until management makes up its mind. Then you must support the decision no matter what your private views on the issue." After hearing this over and over, you have a tendency to respect power and give the god his due. Then, you usually search for the virtues of your idol to avoid losing respect for self. If you worship power alone, you hate yourself, so when a man is put on a pedestal and idolized, the process of making him into a god gets going in earnest. The history of the company is rewritten to make it appear that modern times in the outfit began when he loomed upon the scene. Each plus in the operation is credited to him, whether or not he had anything to do with its birth. He is billed as the heavenly father of all the other leadership and made to look like the only reason these men joined the company. In short, he is given the record to qualify him as a god, worthy of idolatry.

I once took it upon myself to talk to my corporate god about the effect of idolatry on the company he loved with a real measure of godlike devotion that was scarcely visible to the naked eye. My earthly caution to him went something like this:

> These angels of yours have loved you blindly for so long that they don't know you have a new edition of your bible. They do not know that the "god" they serve has changed so much, and you are being used in a form you wouldn't even recognize. Incidentally, though much is different about you now, the eyes of the young see you through the blinded vision of your main disciples, and that's bad.

This statement brought forth a couple of incredulous, deific grunts, and I, the angelic rat that I am, went back to my hole to brush up on my creed and to read again about the meek inheriting the earth. Meanwhile, the everlasting corporate body was chugging along, waiting for god to run his course.

Hooray for the everlasting corporate body. It doesn't have to change its creed to fit its god. Neither does it have to worship by rote as a single person must. Therefore, working quietly without regard to time, it can sip on the creativity of its people to change for the better at an acceptable rate, while I, as a lonesome soul, have to stifle my urge to free-lance my way to corporate glory, as I rise by rote worship to my cloud level selected by the company's one human idol. In the process, I tend to fade away, and the everlasting corporate body makes an ounce of progress every day. One day, from my cloud, I see it sailing by me like a will-o'-the-wisp, as it engulfs all the idols above me. Then I hear the prayers of the fallen idols as they sink into the mist, while surging up from beneath me comes a new god, yelling Geronimo, from the back of a snorting Pegasus. My little piece of everlasting corporate life is over. God is dead, and so am I.

25

START, STUMBLE, AND FALL FORWARD

NEXT TO LIFE itself, man wants a "chance" more than anything else in his world. What good is love, if one doesn't have the chance to feel it? What good is money, if one has no chance to make it or spend it? What good is sex, if one can't find a partner? What good is food, without the chance to eat? What good is music, without the chance to hear it? What good is sowing, without the chance to reap? What good is struggle, without the chance for joyous rest? Over the sounds of cannon, tanks, and bombs in battle, one hears the muffled moan of a G.I. for his buddy, saying, "He didn't have a chance." Back in Kalamazoo, Kankakee, or Kansas City a week later, the dead guy's mother says the same thing as she walks away with a flag in a three-cornered fold—her trophy for eighteen years of nursing a boy to the doorstep of his chance to be a man. I can tell you what a heaven's for. It's to give an individual man or woman another chance. Were this world total in its satisfactions, one would scarcely give a whit for life eternal.

A big business has it over people, for it always gets another chance. Its everlasting corporate body makes it so. Its life is so eternal that utter mismanagement and bankruptcy cannot take away its right to another chance. For the good of humanity, the Penn Central Railroad has to be kept running. Scandals, careless overruns, colossal goofs, and massive mergers are not enough to stomp the breath of lasting life out of giant companies. The 1972 dishonor roll among companies is long, but none will shut its doors nor suffer much. The everlasting corporate body can "start, stumble, and fall forward," without concern for death. Knowing that his starting, stumbling, and falling in this world will be cut short by death, a man has to hope for life on the other side of the grave. It's this weakness of the human body with its repeating need for another chance that brought about the birth of corporations. Long after the individual's happy brush with business opportunity has been stolen by death or ground under the foot of some new god, the company keeps right on starting, stumbling, and falling forward.

Always being able to fall forward is another thing that a big business has over a single man or woman. While man is small enough to blow over backwards, a big company is wind resistant to the point of always falling forward. Even badly managed companies have a lean in the right direction, and their sheer weight keeps them on line when they fall. In bankruptcy, the Penn Central is going down the same tracks, freer of featherbeds and other drains on its energies—falling forward. While tycoons were jumping out of windows in 1929, the everlasting New York Stock Exchange was falling forward to a new understanding of its weaknesses and getting ready to breed another generation of powerful money lords. While Dita Beard was recovering from her heart attack in Denver, I.T.&T. was buying a huge new paper shredder. While Clifford Irving is serving his time for having learned how to write Howard Hughes's name, McGraw-Hill will be conducting a class in how to find a forgery, while falling forward to further success as a respected publisher. In spite of the false starts, the stupid stumbles, and the fatal falls that men in management bring upon themselves as single souls, the companies they mistreat will hold together and prosper.

So clap for big business as it starts, stumbles, and falls forward. No matter what we think of it as part and parcel of the Establishment, it happens to be the source from which most of our individual blessings flow. The small, independent businessman sells his wares to giant companies. Little restaurant owners feed the rats flowing out of big corporations at lunch time. All employees of our mammoth corporate outfits go forth to spend salaries and bonuses all over the lot. Churches, charities, sports, colleges, and governments are all manned by people, sucking on the tit of big business through some straw that's long enough to keep their feet out of the mother cow's crap. Even the Internal Revenue people keep drawing on the milk as they pick her bones. As the slow-moving corporate cow starts, stumbles, and falls forward, she feeds our people from Richard Milhous Nixon to the Blue Angels, in the air and on the ground.

While bigness is not a virtue, it is certainly no sin. If I had the job of standing on the corner of Forty-second Street and Broadway to pass out the interest income of the life insurance company I worked for, it would mean dishing out one hundred thousand dollars an hour for eight hours every working day in the year. Big? You're goddamn right it's big!!! But that money goes into the life blood of this nation every hour by the minute when the cow's on the job. Evil? Hardly!!! It all ends up in somebody's stomach, on somebody's back, or over somebody's head as he sleeps, alone or with another. If not spent for food, clothing, shelter, or companionship, it goes for transportation getting to those things. Before we listen to the hooters on the Hondas, crying, "Shoot the corporate cow," we better have another everlasting generator of life-giving milk. And let's not waste our resources coming up with another source of supply, until we take a look at how we stand on the milk-of-human-kindness as related to how we spread the dairy products of the corporate cow around. We shouldn't kill the cow just because man has a tendency to swap milk and butter for guns. The Russians do the same thing with milk from the big brown bear. Since bears are not good milkers, the Kremlin dairy doesn't have nearly as much for public consumption as does the White House creamery on Pennsylvania Avenue in Washington, D.C.

Maybe we should go to China and get some giant pandas. They ought to have some pretty good milk. Seriously now, welfare families in the U.S. spend more per year on common old ordinary milk than the average Chinese family gets to cover the cost of all its eating, sleeping, clothing, and making love. That old agrarian, Mao Tse-tung, had best stick to row cropping; he's striking out in the milk business. Panda milk is not my idea of nectar. I much prefer milk from a big business cow, even if she's grazing on daisies being pushed up by the bones of frustrated corporate executives who got run down in a race by some god-the-father. Oh, I join with you in deploring the petty practices that clog up the systems of most companies and decrease their worth to the nation, but we must think long and hard about what will take their place, if we the people decide to put them down.

In the hands of imperfect men, any economic system will start, stumble, and hopefully fall forward. Throw out capitalism, with its big business, and the only alternative is some kind of socialism, with its big government. Can you conceive of men in big government playing any fewer games than men in big business? I'd like to know what kind of "corporate" shenanigans go on in that bastion of big government, the Kremlin. Do you reckon there are any teams all-upping back and forth in the ancient halls? While wholly ghosting may be exclusively American, the Kremlin is full of real ghosts wafting around its nooks, led by that old ghost-maker himself, Lavrenti Beria. While nuts in the streets, windows, and hotel basements of our country kill our leaders, at least we don't have a private execution chamber in which we rid ourselves of losing politicians or passed-over corporate bosses. There is sopping in the Kremlin, all right—blood up off the floor. You can bet your bottom ruble that there are games being played in every noncapitalist country. I wonder how tough the rules are and what chance I'd have to be a winner.

If you know the tune to "America the Beautiful," try it on this:

America, America,
God shed his grace on thee.
And wet thy pants
With games of chance,
From sea to shining sea.

Long may be the odds in many cases, but in this less than perfect land of ours, a single soul does have the chance to start where he is, head for better things, stumble over his own feet as well as the trip-cords of others, and make progress as he falls. Compared to most Americans, managers in big business have the best chance to rise and shine, and yet as a group, they may feel more shackled than any other breed. Regardless of education, affluence, and privileges, strong men wilt in the grip of higher power, and only five hundred men have ultimate power in *The Fortune 500* of large corporations. The chance to rise and shine is overshadowed by the slimness of the chance to get a top spot, and frustration sets in. A feeling of futility results, and games get organized to increase one's chances for intermediate power and second-hand glory, if any trickles down from the man on top. As the cigar-store Indian said over and over, "Chance! Chance! Chance!" When taken to task for not saying, "How! How! How!" he screamed, "Know how, want chance!!!"

I have outlined the rules for some of the games we managers play and exposed my own frailties in the face of the "system," if that's what one chooses to call our corporate goings on. I crap you not; in my judgment, I had both the ability and the chance to be the number one man in the outfit. Brother, I knew the rules and could have played a different game. I chose not to, for doing so would have changed me more than I could stand, while making no impact of note on the everlasting corporate body. So let's put the games behind us now and dwell for a few words on what it means to belong to a big company in the truest sense:

> Dangle, dangle, future star,
> Hanging from your thread up thar.
> Touch down here to take your chances;
> A puppet never really dances.
> Your life is fleeting, full of strife;
> I've got the everlasting life.
> Though you be dashing, strong, and brave,
> I will see you to your grave.
> But do not let this moment pass,
> Come on down and bust my ass.
> If you think you're man enough,
> I'll give you a chance to show your stuff.

Out of three important considerations came my chance to howl. One was what the company wanted for itself; two was what the company through its top management wanted for me; three was what I wanted for me. Number one was the company's province. Number three was my domain. Somewhere in number two, we had to find some common ground, if I was going to have any chance at all. We found enough to suit me for my corporate life, and I started strong, rose and shone, stumbled upon a measure of power and glory, and fell forward faster than the company itself for years. When the urge to stop the process hit me, I got out of the pool. You should be so lucky, from start to finish, as I was.

What do you think your chances are? I cannot help you predict your corporate future, but I can tell you about some guys whose odds you've got beat a country mile. Ron Swoboda started with the last-place New York Mets as a clumsy eighteen-year-old, stumbled about the outfield for several seasons, and fell forward in the World Series to help beat Baltimore with a spectacular catch worth a lot of money. Martin Luther King started in the back of a bus, moved to the front to take a chance for human dignity, stumbled on a bridge in Selma as a choice between dogs and sticks, and fell forward on the balcony of a motel in Memphis to give more momentum to civil rights in a decade than Congress had enacted since the Civil War. Charles De Gaulle, like him or not, started with an empire of some significance, stumbled in the control of each outpost, pulled France back within its own boundaries to bring on at least six attempts on his life by French imperialists in the name of patriotism, and fell forward to show the world a new strength in the divesting of power.

Come on in the pool. The water's fine. It's a full-sized, Olympic job with lane markers, starting steps, and electric timers. Not only that, there are teammates, cheerleaders, spectators, and coaches to add spice to your life. You can stay out of the deep end if you wish, but after you learn to swim, you can go off the high board. Competition will be as keen as you make it, and contrary to public opinion, no one is going to drown you if you keep your eyes open. If you start and stumble off the step, you ll, at worst, fall forward into the water. If you don't like the games we play in the pool of big business, climb back up your thread of life and dangle down in some other tank, but don't forget, the water you'll find there will have been siphoned off from the reservoir belonging to America's giants with the everlasting corporate life, from which flow all liquids essential to human beings in our society.

Recommended Readings

HERE IS A SAMPLE of the kind of extra reading you might do to make *Working Your Way Up the Corporation* more meaningful to you:

From cover to cover:

> *Up the Organization*—Robert Townsend
> Alfred A. Knopf, New York, 1970
>
> *The Peter Principle*—Laurence F. Peter
> William Morrow, New York, 1969
>
> *The Effective Executive*—Peter Ferdinand Drucker
> Harper & Row, New York, 1967

I feel strongly that reading *Working Your Way Up the Corporation* will make these books more interesting and more helpful to a man or woman sitting in the catbird seat of management.

For selected chapters:

> *On Becoming a Corporate Ace*—Malcolm Kent
> Laddin Press, New York, 1972
> Chapter 2, "The Plight of the Super Bright, Live Wires in Dead Companies"

The Mobile Manager—Eugene Emerson Jennings
University of Michigan Press, Ann Arbor, 1967
Chapter V, "The Shelf Sitter"

The Pyramid Climbers—Vance Packard
McGraw-Hill, New York, 1962
Chapter 2, "The Pyramids and the Climbers"

Managing the Managers—Robert C. Sampson
McGraw-Hill, New York, 1965
Chapter 8, "Power in Organizations"

Managing Through Insight—Staff of Rohrer, Hibler, & Replogle
World Publishing, New York, 1968
Chapter 13, "The Inside Talent Hunt"

About the Author

CHARLES R. MURRAH was born in Shiloh, Georgia, on December 7, 1917, and grew up in Pine Mountain. After two years at the University of Alabama and one at Marion Military Institute, he entered West Point in 1937 and graduated in June 1941.

Five years in the army followed, during which Murrah served in four combat campaigns in Europe, winning the Silver Star and Bronze Star. He resigned in 1946 to become commandant of Marion Institute, where he stayed for two years. Then came one year in public relations for Centenary College, Shreveport, Louisiana, before starting to sell life insurance in that city in 1949, with Mutual of New York.

After becoming the company's agency manager in Kansas City, he entered the home office in New York City in 1958, rose to regional vice president in 1961 and to second vice president for manpower and merchandising in 1965. Promoted to vice president for merchandising in 1967, he became vice president for sales administration in 1970 and then vice president for corporate projects in 1971. At the end of 1972, he retired at age fifty-five to seek a new life in sales training and management training.

He has written several articles for insurance publications and wrote "How to Stay on Top of Your Job," for *Nation's Business* in the September 1971 issue.

Mr. Murrah and his wife have two grown daughters, and live in New York.